S0-DNI-291

LITTLE WOMEN

BY
KATE HAMILL

ADAPTED FROM THE NOVEL BY
LOUISA MAY ALCOTT

★

★

DRAMATISTS
PLAY SERVICE
INC.

LITTLE WOMEN
Copyright © 2021, Kate Hamill

All Rights Reserved

LITTLE WOMEN is fully protected under the copyright laws of the United States of America, and of all countries covered by the International Copyright Union (including the Dominion of Canada and the rest of the British Commonwealth), and of all countries covered by the Pan-American Copyright Convention, the Universal Copyright Convention, the Berne Convention, and of all countries with which the United States has reciprocal copyright relations. No part of this publication may be reproduced in any form by any means (electronic, mechanical, photocopying, recording, or otherwise), or stored in any retrieval system in any way (electronic or mechanical) without written permission of the publisher.

The stock and amateur stage performance rights throughout the world for LITTLE WOMEN are controlled exclusively by Dramatists Play Service, 440 Park Avenue South, New York, NY 10016. **No professional or nonprofessional performance of the Play may be given without obtaining in advance the written permission of Dramatists Play Service and paying the requisite fee.**

All other rights, including without limitation motion picture, recitation, lecturing, public reading, radio broadcasting, television, video or sound recording, and the rights of translation into foreign languages are strictly reserved.

Inquiries concerning all other rights should be addressed to APA Agency, 3 Columbus Circle, 23rd Floor, New York, NY 10019. Attn: Beth Blickers.

NOTE ON BILLING
Anyone receiving permission to produce LITTLE WOMEN is required to give credit to the Author as sole and exclusive Author of the Play on the title page of all programs distributed in connection with performances of the Play and in all instances in which the title of the Play appears, including printed or digital materials for advertising, publicizing or otherwise exploiting the Play and/or a production thereof. Please see your production license for font size and typeface requirements.

Be advised that there may be additional credits required in all programs and promotional material. Such language will be listed under the "Additional Billing" section of production licenses. It is the licensee's responsibility to ensure any and all required billing is included in the requisite places, per the terms of the license.

SPECIAL NOTE ON SONGS/RECORDINGS
Dramatists Play Service neither holds the rights to nor grants permission to use any songs or recordings mentioned in the Play. Permission for performances of copyrighted songs, arrangements or recordings mentioned in this Play is not included in our license agreement. The permission of the copyright owner(s) must be obtained for any such use. For any songs and/or recordings mentioned in the Play, other songs, arrangements, or recordings may be substituted provided permission from the copyright owner(s) of such songs, arrangements or recordings is obtained; or songs, arrangements or recordings in the public domain may be substituted.

Dedicated to my mother, Monica Joyce Hamill,
who gave me Little Women *when I was very young—*
and who always wanted me to find my own
definition of being a "woman."

LITTLE WOMEN was commissioned and originally produced by the Jungle Theater (Sarah Rasmussen, Artistic Director), Minneapolis, Minnesota, in September 2018. It was directed by Sarah Rasmussen, the set design was by Chelsea M. Warren, the costume design was by Rebecca Bernstein, the lighting design was by Marcus Dilliard, the sound design was by Sean Healey, the original music was by Robert Elhai, the dramaturg was Kristin Leahey, and the production stage manager was John Novak. The cast was as follows:

MARMEE MARCH .... Christina Baldwin
MEG MARCH .... Christine Weber
JO MARCH .... C. Michael Menge
BETH MARCH .... Isabella Star LaBlanc
AMY MARCH .... Megan Burns
HANNAH/MRS. MINGOTT/AUNT MARCH .... Wendy Lehr
LAURIE .... Michael Hanna
MR. LAURENCE/MR. DASHWOOD .... Jim Lichtscheidl
JOHN BROOKS .... James Rodríguez
MR. MARCH/MUSICIAN .... Tyson Forbes

LITTLE WOMEN received its New York City premiere at Primary Stages (Andrew Leynse, Artistic Director; Shane D. Hudson, Executive Director; Casey Childs, Founder), at the Cherry Lane Theatre in June 2019. It was directed by Sarna Lapine, the set design was by Mikiko Suzuki MacAdams, the costume design was by Valérie Thérèse Bart, the lighting design was by Paul Whitaker, the sound design was by Leon Rothenberg, the original music was by Deborah Abramson, the dramaturg was Kristin Leahey, and the production stage manager was Bonnie McHeffey. The cast was as follows:

MARMEE MARCH/AUNT MARCH .... Maria Elena Ramirez
MEG MARCH .... Kate Hamill
JO MARCH .... Kristolyn Lloyd
BETH MARCH .... Paola Sanchez Abreu
AMY MARCH .... Carmen Zilles
HANNAH/MRS. MINGOTT/MESSENGER .... Ellen Harvey
LAURIE .... Nate Mann
JOHN BROOKS/PARROT/MR. DASHWOOD .... Michael Crane
MR. LAURENCE/ROBERT MARCH/DOCTOR .... John Lenartz

LITTLE WOMEN was developed at the Colorado New Play Festival, Steamboat Springs, Colorado, in June 2018.

It was also developed at the Playwrights' Center in Minneapolis in September 2017.

My especial thanks to Kristin Leahey for her eagle-eyed dramaturgy!
—K.H.

CHARACTER BREAKDOWN

Doubling for 9 actors.

Women

ACTOR 1

MARMEE MARCH. The matriarch of the March family. A social revolutionary, ahead of her time. Good sense of humor. A warrior; keeps the family together. Tough. Strong. Intelligent.

AUNT MARCH. (70+) The most unpleasant old woman imaginable. Has lots of money; privileged. Strong political and personal opinions, which people endure. Judgmental. Has an intermittent, hacking, disgusting cough.

ACTOR 2

MEG MARCH. The oldest March daughter. Wears glasses. Acts as Marmee's second in the house. A romantic at heart—likes to dress up and have little luxuries in life.

ACTOR 3

JO MARCH. The second-oldest March. Does not fit comfortably within the parameters of her given gender role. A deep fire within her. Extremely ambitious and frustrated by the distance between where she is and where she wants to be. Impatient. Wants to change the world. Very smart and knows it. A mix of insecurity and aspiration. Boyish and rough-and-tumble. Sometimes antagonistic. Not the most tolerant of differing viewpoints. Can be quite awkward or abrupt; bad temper when riled. A great sense of humor. Passionate. Ahead of her time. A warrior. Has a special relationship with Beth.

ACTOR 4

BETH MARCH. The third March. An extremely special person. Very sweet and paralytically shy; had to be removed from school because of her paralyzing social anxieties. Agoraphobic. Almost incapable of going out in the world; sheltered by her family. Loves deeply and has deep empathy for everyone. Loves the simple things in life—so much that it hurts. Sees much more than anyone realizes. Brave and sensitive; quick to forgive and heal wounds. An observer.

AMY MARCH. The youngest March. Opinionated and spunky; popular and quite focused on style. Not the most tolerant of differing viewpoints. Socially intelligent. Sometimes puts on airs. Perhaps a bit spoiled. A perfect little lady—except for her temper, and her not-so-great command of "vocabiblary." Grows up to be quite beautiful and elegant. Madly in love with Laurie, around whom she is never cool.

ACTOR 6

HANNAH. Irish. The March's longtime housekeeper, cook, and de facto babysitter. A treasure; a terror; a traditionalist. Takes no nonsense. Matter-of-fact; she's the boss of that kitchen, for sure.

MRS. MINGOTT. A very rich, stylish woman. Vanderbilt-esque, condescending, not terribly pleasant; fancies herself charitable.

MESSENGER. A female messenger.

Men

ACTOR 7

THEODORE "LAURIE" LAURENCE. A sweet and handsome young man. Sensitive. Funny, charming, and caring. In his fantasies he's a white knight: riding in to rescue damsels in distress. A natural musician. Wealthy thanks to his inheritance; generous, does not have to think about money. Does not always fit comfortably within the parameters of his given gender role—he doesn't want to grow up to be a soldier or tedious man of business. Finds a family in the Marches.

ACTOR 8

JOHN BROOKS. Laurie's sometimes stiff and awkward tutor. A rule follower. A poor man, well educated. Has a very noticeable limp—probably served in the war and was sent home, although may have been disqualified from service altogether. Feels deeply. Quite madly in love with Meg.

PARROT. Aunt March's parrot: pure evil. A musty, disgusting bird. Probably an actual demon in parrot form.

MR. LAURENCE. Laurie's grandfather, responsible for Laurie's upbringing. A wealthy man. A gentleman in the strictest sense. Not comfortable with emotional language; bad at expressing himself. Has a rigid sense of what is appropriate behavior, especially for a man. Tends towards gruffness or temper. Probably quite unintentionally frightening. Deeply regretful of incidents in his past, but unable to express it.

ROBERT MARCH. Father to the March girls. Never speaks, but his presence looms large. Wounded in the war; never quite recovers. A significant limp. Struggles with his injuries, both emotional and physical.

Actor 8 or Actor 9 will also double the part of:

MR. DASHWOOD. A publisher of cheap newspapers and novels. A businessman, working in a man's world. Fancies himself a realist. Not a nice guy. Fancies himself a nice guy.

DOCTOR *(nonspeaking)*

IMPORTANT NOTES

—*Little Women* MUST be cast in an inclusive fashion—particularly the March family. It is an American play and should reflect America today.

—In the March household, in this play, there is not much room for expressing grief openly and fully—perhaps because in times like these, you might fear that if you let it out, it will never stop coming. Often when we cannot express sadness, we turn to anger/aggression.

—The trap in this play—and all plays have traps—is to try to recreate the novel, or some idea of the novel, or some idea of the archetypes found in the novel. This adaptation is a retelling, and in some ways a conscious explosion of those archetypes. It is not polite. None of the characters are good or bad. They are not always likable—and that's particularly important for young women, the freedom to not be "likable" at all times—but they are human. They are imperfect people, and it is not a perfect family.

A slash / in a line of dialogue indicates where the next character should begin speaking.

Parentheses around dialogue mean the words are not necessarily heard by the audience.

LITTLE WOMEN

ACT ONE

Scene 1

Over the set hangs a Civil War-era photograph of the March girls—on the cusp of being March women. A clock below the portrait ticks. Jo is writing in a red notebook. She is in a masculine outfit—her father's castoffs. Beth sits by Jo's desk, examining a flower. Here and there may be homely pots of flowers—well taken care of, but not too showy.

BETH. Tell me a story, Jo.

JO. *(Still writing.)* Now?

   Beth nods. Jo pastes on a bad mustache.

Once upon a time, there was a WIZARD named RODRIGO, and he cast a TERRIBLE / (SPELL)

BETH. —not that kind of story.

JO. That's what I'm writing, Beth… *(Assuming a big, masculine Rodrigo voice.)* RODRIGO AND HIS DASTARDLY DEEDS of DEPRAVITY! In this chapter, he finds a beautiful, Scantily Clad, SCREAMING maiden, tied up to an ENORMOUS / (worm)

BETH. —A REAL one.

JO. Those are boring.

   Beth stares at her expectantly. She may even pointedly clear her throat. Jo tries to ignore Beth, then—

Once upon a time, there was a little girl, who was being a pest.

BETH. Her name was Beth.

JO. And this little girl had a monster of a sister—

BETH. *(Objecting.)* Jo!

JO. —that's right, its name was Jo!

BETH. And Beth liked her monster very much. And?

JO. And there were two other sisters in there somewhere. And a mother, and a father.

She takes off the mustache and fiddles with it.

And this family lived in a small house in the shadows of a big city. And outside the city was an even bigger country—

BETH. And that country went to war.

JO. To war with itself.

But even though the father went to fight—

BETH. That was hard—

JO. —even if the world had split apart—that little girl and her monster: together, they felt whole.

BETH. What happened when they grew up?

JO. In this story, they never grow up. They just stay the same, and it lasts forever.

BETH. Nothing lasts forever, Jo.
Tell it again?

Offstage, a dinner bell rings. Both sit up—this means breakfast.

AMY. *(Off.)* —but I don't WANT to—

Jo may be about to get out of her masculine outfit and into a skirt draped over her chair—but, swiftly, reconsiders—pastes on the mustache again, and exits.

BETH. Jo!

Beth follows her into breakfast as we transition to:

12

Scene 2

Breakfast in the March household. December, 1861. Amy sits. Meg is doing her hair.

AMY. But I don't WANT to, Meg!

MEG. You're too young to turn your hair up, Amy!

HANNAH. *(Off.)* MISS AMY, YER NOT WEARING NOTHING BUT BRAIDS, YOU'RE TOO LITTLE!

AMY. I'M NOT LITTLE, HANNAH! I am PRACTICABLY A FULL-GROWN WOMAN!

> *Hannah barks laughter from the kitchen. Jo has entered in her mustachioed costume, Beth behind her.*

—I'm more of a woman than Jo, anyway! *(Re: her hair being braided.)* OW!

> *Hannah enters, slams down a plate of breakfast—turns and sees Jo. An unpleasant moment.*

JO. *(With false innocence.)* —what?

HANNAH. *(Darkly.)* Yer hands clean at least?

> *Jo turns up her hands, which are covered with ink.*

MEG. Ink! Again!

JO. I was writing my play! / I must chase my inspiration in the morning before Aunt March breaks my spirit.

HANNAH. *(Under to Meg, re: Jo's outfit.)* You gonna do something about this?

BETH. Where is Marmee, Hannah?

MEG. *(Under to Hannah.)* What am I supposed to do?

HANNAH. Some creature came begging and your ma went off to see what was needed.

> *She bustles away.*

MEG. Why are you wearing the costume, Jo? We're not rehearsing today.

JO. I'm man of the family, with Father away!

AMY. Josephine is so childish, Meg. It is most aggregating.

MEG. (Amy—)

JO. "Aggregating"! That's a new one.

She pulls out a red notebook and writes it down.

MEG. You mean "aggravating," dear.

JO. "Aggregating."   AMY. Ow—

AMY. So what, Jo? A lady should seek to improve her vocabiblary.

JO. Vocabiblary!

AMY. Stop writing them down!

Jo holds up her book and flips the pages.

JO. Someday, I shall publish the collection!

AMY. You won't!

JO. Will.

AMY. Won't—Josephine.

JO. Will—!

AMY. WON'T—JOSEPHINE.

HANNAH. *(Entering, slams down the syrup.)* GIRLS. EAT. Soldiers are starving in the field!

The girls eat.

JO. *(Sighing as she takes enormous helpings of food.)* I have no appetite.

BETH. Poor Jo. It must be hard to wait on Aunt March all day.

JO. *(Mouth full.)* Torchewr.

She picks mustache out of mouth.

But come the new year, she'll take me to EUROPE!

She bangs on the table in a drumroll of excitement; they all have to steady cups.

MEG. I'd a thousand times rather sit with Aunt March than be the Mingotts' governess, with Mrs. Mingott— *(Putting on a Mingott air.)* of the Manhattan Mingotts—always talking down to me.

BETH. Poor Meg.

AMY. At least neither of you have to go to school, the days are quite intermintable—

JO. *(Pulls out book.)* "Intermintable"!

BETH. Poor Amy—

AMY. —girls laugh at my braids, and sniff because we're poor, and label Papa for being an abolitionist—

JO. "Libel." Labels are for pickle bottles.

MEG. We all got through school,   AMY. *(To Meg.)* OW!
Amy, and you'll survive it, too.

AMY. Not Beth! Why did she get to stay home?

> *Amy's really crossed a line; Meg may smack her a little, lightly—Beth quails under the attention.*

BETH. Because I am—stupid.

JO. *(Very very angry.)* Beth had nervous episodes!

AMY. I'M NERVOUS!

MEG. Amy, hush!

AMY. Why does she get one thing and me another?

MEG. Different people need different things.

JO. And you need to go to school—for you have a terrible case of the Moron!

MEG. JO—

JO. —I don't know that it's curable!

AMY. You—YOU'RE THE MORON, YOU STUPID INKY STUPID OLD STUPID JOSEPHINE STUPID! When I grow up I am going to run away with a—a prince, that's all!

JO. "That's all!"   AMY. And I DON'T need school
                                                    for that—

AMY. —and I shall NEVER spoil MY hands with working!

JO. My hands are inky because I am going to be a great writer and make my mark upon the world!

> *She jumps up on the table to general consternation—"Jo, Jo!" etc.*[*]

—and then I'll buy Meg all the dresses she wants and you spelling primers—

---

[*] See overlapping dialogue at end of script.

15

Amy reacts badly.

—and Beth, what can I get you, a whole hothouse of flowers?!

BETH. All I want is the family I have, you bad Jo.

AMY. How are *you* going to become a famous writer? You're just a penniless girl with a nasty temper and a pasted-on mustache. Really, Josephine, you are positively *(The killing stroke.)* de-lusual!

MEG. ..."Delusional."

JO. In a couple of weeks, I'm going to EUROPE! And that's where I'll find the way to make my fortune!

AMY. *(Jealously.)* Oh, Europe. Europe Europe Europe. Nobody CARES!

JO. You're just jealous.

AMY. *(Outraged.)* Jealous!

JO. You'll see! In Europe, I'll become Shakespeare and Dickens and Thackeray ALL! IN! ONE!

> *She makes a big, sweeping gesture and knocks over a cup of coffee.*

Oop!

> *Amy gives a little feminine scream of dismay as the liquid rolls over the table towards her.* * *Beth cleans it up.*
>
> *The sound of a bell—the front door is opening. Jo hurriedly hops off the table.*

MARMEE. Hello, girls!

> *Jo mouths "delusual" at Amy and writes it down as Marmee enters and takes off her coat, brushing snow off.*

BETH. Marmee!

> *Beth runs and embraces her.*

MARMEE. Mustachios, Jo? It's early for the theater.

> *Jo kisses her mother on the cheek.*

Ouch.

BETH. Where were you?

MARMEE. Do you remember that immigrant woman with the baby:

---

* See overlapping dialogue at end of script.

Mrs. Hummel? Her little boy came begging. I went with him and found Mrs. Hummel terribly ill, with her children crying from hunger, in conditions—

She stops, overwhelmed.

Well. I tried to help.

BETH. Poor Marmee.

MARMEE. I've been thinking, girls: Christmas is almost here, but it's a hard winter for so many, with the war. Perhaps we shouldn't spend for pleasure. With Father away we can't do much, but we can make some sacrifices. We each can play our part.

General dismay.

MEG. No Christmas?!

MARMEE. We'll be together, and we'll have Jo's theatrical! But perhaps no presents.
You are becoming adults. That means learning what you need— and what you don't.

Silence.

It is only a proposal.

AMY. Christmas without any presents!

MEG. Oh, Marmee, it does seem so—

JO. —SAD! Does the war have to take everything?

BETH. They work so hard, Marmee.

JO. Beth does too, she does so much at home—

AMY. And me at school—

MEG. Maybe no presents, Marmee.

Amy gives a little scream.

But we each have a dollar! Perhaps we could just…spend it on ourselves!

Amy gives a little, slightly happy, scream.

JO. Can't we buy just what we really want?

AMY. What we really NEED?

Pause.

MARMEE. All right, girls.

She waves a soiled white table napkin in mock defeat.

I surrender.

BETH. I'm going to buy YOU something with my dollar, Marmee—a, a real treat.

MARMEE. I have enough.

    The girls get ready to go.

HANNAH. *(Manhandling her apron, full of hot potatoes.)* Girls! It's Potato O'Clock.
(Pointedly.) Miss Jo.

JO. What?

MARMEE. Jo. *(Referencing her outfit.)* You know you can't.

    *Jo is forced to don her skirt. She reluctantly pulls off her mus-
    tache and deposits it in Hannah's hand. Maybe they all watch
    this as they pull on hats, coats; they do not comment on it.*

MEG. *(In her best martial bellow.)* PREE-SENT!

MARMEE. Marches… march!

    *Jo salutes. The girls march out, singing "The Battle Hymn of the
    Republic." As they do: Hannah hands them each a hot potato to
    keep their fingers warm. Amy refuses her potato with a shake of
    the head and a sniff. Jo, rolling her eyes, takes two, as they sing:*

MARCH GIRLS.
    Glory Glory Hallelujah
    Glory Glory Hallelujah
    Glory Glory Hallelujah
    His Truth is marching on!

Scene 3

    They stop just outside the front door, wincing with the cold.

AMY. Meg—do you have a dime?

JO. Potato.

AMY. A dime for limes, Meg, I'm dreadfully in debt.

18

JO. Potato, Amy.

AMY. It's hot!

JO. That's the point.

AMY. I owe a dozen pickled limes to the other girls at school—for if one girl likes another, she gives her a lime, and I've gotten *so* many but haven't returned any, and soon I shall become a piranha!

JO. Pariah.

> *She pulls out her book, writes "piranha" down.*

MEG. Jo.

JO. Why don't you spend your Christmas dollar on limes?

AMY. I shall be using my dollar to buy a muff, Josephine—so I never shall have to carry a dirty hot potato ever again! Besides, that money is to buy something for *ourselves*, not for others!

MEG. —I know we ought to give up presents gladly, but I'm just not that good.

JO. We ought to do many things—

MEG. —we ought to be grateful! After all, we have Father and Marmee and each other.

AMY. *(Juggling with the hot potato.)* We haven't got Father and won't for a long time. Perhaps— *(Getting upset.)* ow—perhaps never.

JO. Don't say that!

AMY. *(Quite upset.)* And my dollar can't bring him back, can it!

> *She angrily takes it out on the potato, dropping it with a dull thud.*

So I'm getting myself a muff!

> *She almost cries.*

MEG. Amy—

> *Amy sniffles a little and hides her face in Meg's coat. Piano music plays. After a moment, Amy lifts her face and listens, distracted.*

JO. What's that?

MEG. Hannah said Mr. Laurence's grandson moved in next door. His parents died.

JO. He sure can play.

They listen for a moment.

AMY. It's sad.

JO. An orphan, growing up alone in that big house—you'd be sad, too.

MEG. He has a tutor, Hannah said, and his grandfather.

JO. You can be lonely in a crowd, if it's not the right crowd.

Jo, stuffing her hand in her pockets, begins whistling along with the music—

AMY. Don't, Jo—it's so boyish.

Jo whistles even louder. The music stops. Jo whistles the next part. The piano responds. They duet for a minute. Then it stops. A shadow comes to the window. Jo raises a hand to wave—the shadow slowly raises its hand, mirroring her. Another shadow comes to the window and pulls the first one away. The girls turn to go.

Meg, my dime? My dime, Meg? My dime?

Meg fishes out a dime. Amy skips off, singing. Jo picks up Amy's discarded potato.

JO. POTATO!

Maybe she chucks the potato after Amy, football-style; however it happens, Amy has escaped.

AMY. (*Off, singing to the tune of "Battle Hymn."*) Limes! Limes! Limeslimeslimeslimes—

JO. You never would have given *me* a dime, in our school days.

MEG. Don't be jealous.

JO. Me—jealous of *Amy*?!

MEG. Time for work, Josephine.

Jo makes a face. Meg exits—Jo pauses, still staring at the window.

(*Off.*) Jo!

Jo exits.

Scene 4

A repetition of Amy's little song from offstage: "Limes, Limes, Limeslimeslimes"—and then a hard sound of a SLAP! Amy screams offstage—and then runs onstage. She runs until she's almost home, is about to go inside—but hesitates outside. She sits on a snowbank and feels sorry for herself. Laurie, a handsome, sweet young man, comes out to the mailbox with a letter.

LAURIE. Oh! Hello!

> *Amy cries hysterically.*

—Are you all right?

> *She cries.*

—I say, miss, are you all right?

AMY. Leave me alone! LEAVE ME ALONE TO DIE IN THE SNOWWWWWW!

> *She throws herself down and sobs into the snow.*

LAURIE. —Come, what's the matter?

AMY. *(Cries.)* —I can't say, it's too shameful!

LAURIE. *(Improvising.)* Well—sure. A damsel in distress should retain an air of mystery.

> *He offers her a hankie.*

You're one of the March girls, aren't you?
I've been watching—seeing you all. I'm Theodore Laurence. *(Laurie doesn't have any friends:)* But my friends call me Laurie.

> *He holds out a hand to shake.*

AMY. Laurie Laurence? That's terrible. *(Sniffs.)* Why not Theodore?

LAURIE. It's just not who I am.

> *Pause.*

—Don't you want to go indoors?

AMY. Nobody understands in there.

LAURIE. Truly? You all seem so happy together. I mean, when I happen to—to see you.

AMY. They tease and scold me and think I'm spoilt!

NO no—nobody even TRIES to understand me ANYWHERE!

> *She wails again.*

LAURIE. —I'm trying.

> *She looks at him and sniffs.*

AMY. Well—I owed a dozen pickled limes to the other girls at school, you see—

LAURIE. Of course—

AMY. —for if one girl likes another, she gives her a lime, and I was becoming a piranha—

LAURIE. Naturally—

AMY. And—and Mr. Smith caught me passing a lime—

LAURIE. The scoundrel—

AMY. —and he brought me to the front of the room and he took a rod and he—he WHACKED me!

LAURIE. Shall I kill him for you?

AMY. Yes please.

> *Amy holds out her hand, which is red.*

It's all red and hot.

> *He carefully blows on her hand a little.*

LAURIE. —better?

> *Amy nods and wipes her tears. From the Laurences' house, Brooks, Laurie's tutor, enters. He can't see Amy until he's almost upon them.*

BROOKS. *(Quite angry and frustrated.)* Theodore Laurence, you cannot escape your lessons forever!—Oh

> *He stops short, uncomfortable—he's not good with children.*

What is—that?

LAURIE. It's the neighbors' little girl, Brooks.

BROOKS. —Hello, uh—Neighbor's Little Girl. / Have you—hurt, or…

AMY. I am NOT a little girl, I'm NOT—

BROOKS. *(Reacting to the meltdown.)* all right—Just bring her to her parents—

AMY. —I AM A FULL-GROWN WOMAN!

She sits on the snowbank and starts sobbing, this time straight into Laurie's handkerchief.

Brooks looks at Laurie—he clearly doesn't have it handled. Brooks marches up to the Marches' door and knocks. Laurie attempts to console a sobbing Amy.

BROOKS. Theodore, you have Latin!!!!

As he knocks quite hard, the door swings open on Brooks—it's Meg; she's been doing housework and is wiping her hands on an apron. Brooks looks at her, stunned—his hand keeps knocking on empty air.

MEG. Yes?

Long pause.

Can I help you?

Brooks is finally able to stop knocking but cannot speak.

LAURIE. —I, uh, found a damsel in distress upon your snowbank.

Jo has crowded behind Meg, Beth behind Jo.

MEG. Amy, what are you doing here?!!!!

JO. Christopher Columbus, why aren't you in school?!!

Beth heads towards Amy and wordlessly touches her, consoling. Amy bursts into even noisier tears.

MEG. Please excuse us, Mr.—

Brooks cannot speak. Beth holds on to Amy, supporting her into the house.

AMY. I want to talk to Marmee—

MEG. Mr.—?

AMY. *(Really sobbing.)* I WANT TO TALK TO Marmee!

MEG. Please excuse us!

Meg shuts the door quickly, leaving Jo outside; the slam brings Brooks back to life.

BROOKS. Brooks. John Brooks.

He stands staring at the door.

LAURIE. *(Gesturing after Amy with the handkerchief she dropped.)* She may need this.

JO. *(Friendly; taking the hankie.)* If she's the damsel in distress, you must be the knight in shining armor?

> *Laurie makes a fake blow of a trumpet's charge.*

BROOKS. Theodore!… Latin. *(Reminding himself.)* LATIN!

> *Brooks staggers back towards the Laurence house. Laurie pulls a face, whistles as he goes in—the tune Jo whistled to him at the piano.*

MEG. *(Offstage.)* Jo!

> *Jo goes inside.*

Scene 5

> *Amy sits crying. Beth massages Amy's slapped hand—Meg consoles. Jo hangs back a bit, after handing off the hankie to Meg with raised eyebrows.*

MARMEE. There's enough violence in the country without men hitting little girls.

AMY. I'm not a little girl!

MARMEE. You can take leave from school for now, Amy—

AMY. Huzzah!

MARMEE. —and be tutored by me at home, instead.

AMY. Oh.

MARMEE. "Oh." And no limes in my classroom.

MEG. Let's wash your face.

> *She leads Amy out of the room.*

JO. Marmee, we all had to survive school—why shouldn't she?

MARMEE. You liked school.

BETH. I got to stay home, Jo.

JO. Yes, Beth, but you're—you're my conscience, is what you are,

24

and Amy is terribly spoilt. What kind of lesson will she learn?

MARMEE. —Look at Beth's flowers, will you?

JO. Marmee, please—no analogies.

MARMEE. Here's a violet: How do we care for it, Beth?

BETH. They like things calm—not too hot or cold. And they like the shade of other plants, so we pot them with their relations.

MARMEE. And here's a rose: What does it need?

BETH. You have to put it where sun is! And it's delicate; you have to give it support, or it won't thrive.

JO. Ow.

BETH. —thorns.

MARMEE. The rose would wilt if she gave it the care of another flower, and the violet too. One isn't better than the other. They just need different things to grow.

JO. So if Beth is a violet—

BETH. *(Surprised.)* Oh!

JO. And Amy a rose—what is Meg?

BETH. *(Delighted to play the game.)* A—Daisy! She bloomed before all the others!

JO. Then I am… Moss. Dirt. *(Snaps.)* A rock.

MARMEE. You are—whatever you're supposed to be.
Look at them: Aren't they beautiful together?

> *Meg and Amy return; Amy's hand is wrapped in a comically large bandage.*

MEG. The wound is salved—with Mr. Laurence's hankie, no less.

AMY. His NAME is LAURIE.

JO. Laurie Laurence? That's terrible.

MARMEE. I want to hear all about him, and about the rest of your days—so wash up for dinner.

MEG. Speaking of my day, Jo—the Mingotts invited us to their dance this weekend.

> *Amy GASPS with extreme delight. Meg stares at Jo.*

JO. Oh no. No nonono—

MEG. You MUST come with me, Jo—

AMY. *(Waving her hand; ripping off her bandage, miraculously healed.)* I will, I will—

MEG. You're too little, Amy!

JO. Meg—
No, no no—I work all the time and I want to have an evening in—

AMY. ERNGH!!!!

MEG. Jo, I work all the time and I want to have an evening out—and you know I can't go unchaperoned—

MEG. And we're growing up now, and that means we must appear in society! I want it—I NEED it so much! PLEASE?!!!

Jo looks at Marmee.

JO. —But I'm the rock.

Amy stomps off. They transition into the ball. Meg nervously adjusts herself.

Scene 6

The ballroom of Mrs. Mingott—of the Manhattan Mingotts. Meg and Jo—aware that they are considered charity cases— are on painful, conscious, anxious display here.

MEG. Do I look all right?

JO. Don't ask me for womanish opinions, Meg, I never say the right thing.

MEG. Just keep it simple, as: "Oh, Jo, your hair looks so well."

JO. *(She's bad at this.)* Oh, Meg, I—like—your…dress.

MEG. *(Playing with it.)* Marmee says I may have a silk when I am married—but I'll be so old by the time that happens!

JO. I should hope so. *(Off of Meg's look.)* —What?

MEG. Why are you holding your pop* like that?

JO. There's a rip in the seat.

---

* "Pop" is short for "poplin," the fabric used for the March sisters' dresses.

MEG. Can't you hold your gloves over it?

JO. I spilled lemonade on 'em.

MEG. And WHAT is THIS?

JO. A burn. I think.

MEG. Jo, just—stand against the wall, so nobody sees you. But don't put your hands behind you. Or say "Christopher Columbus." Or stare, or bounce, or breathe—(or)

JO. MEG! Tell you what: if you see me doing anything wrong, give me a poke.

MEG. Poking isn't ladylike. I'll give a cough! Like this—

She gives a horrible, hideous cough.

JO. —really?

MEG. —here comes Mrs. Mingott! Jo— *(Fluttering.)* —just stand there normally—

Jo lounges, whistling.

NOT normally! NOT NORMALLY, JO. APPROPRIATELY.

MRS. MINGOTT. Miss Josephine!

Jo salutes bouncily; Meg coughs frantically.

And dear Miss March!

Meg is still hacking away at Jo.

—are you all right?

MEG. Oh! Yes.

MRS. MINGOTT. The governess at the ball! *(This is not a good thing:)* And my heavens, don't you look…smart.

MEG. Thank you?

MRS. MINGOTT. Cinderella before the godmother! Well, poof— here I am: I'll make a princess yet. Oop, *(Adjusts Meg invasively.)* there, there, *(Looks at Meg's glasses.)* no— *(Steals them.)* —and put THESE, just—so— *(Pushes Meg's dress down so her bosom is far more exposed.)* Alakazam.

Jo whistles—not a good whistle. Meg, barely able to see, looks down at her exposed décolletage.

MEG. Oh!

MRS. MINGOTT. Now stay right there.

She flips up her fan and sails away, commanding:

STAY!

JO. Meg, you can't see without your glasses!

MEG. I can so!

JO. How many fingers am I holding up?

MEG. Don't be ridiculous!

She reaches out to slap the fingers down and misses entirely.

JO. You're blind!!! *Half-naked* and blind.

MEG. Don't talk to me like I'm Amy, Josephine, I am your elder, and what's more, I am ACTING like a LADY!

She flips open her fan, and, blind, hits herself in the face with it.

Ow.

She gropes her way to a wall, then stands. Jo holds her up.

MRS. MINGOTT. Miss March, Miss Marrrrch! Look, Cinderella—I have conjured up a wobbly old Prince!

They bow/curtsy; Meg barely makes it back up.

JO. It's Mr. Brooks, Meg.

Meg, who can't see, has no idea who that is.

MEG. *(Mouthing it, unvoiced.)* (Who?)

JO. The Laurence boy's tutor.

MRS. MINGOTT. As Miss March is our *governess*, you two should have PLENTY to talk about— *(Struggling to come up with what that is.)* lesson plans, and trigonometry, and—and chalk. I insist that you fearsome scholars take a turn about the room, now! Oop!

She gives an additional tug to Meg's bosom.

BROOKS. Madame.

Meg, quite bewildered, curtsies. Still blind, grasps his arm, and is led away onto the dance floor. Mrs. Mingott backs Jo against the wall.

MRS. MINGOTT. And Miss Josephine! Hm hm hm HM.

She sizes her up, disdainfully, punctuating each "hm" by hitting imagined flaws with Meg's glasses.

28

(Darkly.) I'll dig up some creature for *you*, somehow—some way. *(Jo grabs Meg's glasses.)* You stay right there! STAY!

> *Mrs. Mingott marches away. Jo, horrified, slides against the wall, trying not to be caught moving, until she reaches a curtained recess. She escapes inside—to find Laurie, who is also hiding.*

JO. Oh!—please excuse me!

> *She prepares to back out as speedily as she bounced in. They're very awkward.*

LAURIE. No! Stay.—and I'll go.

> *He starts to leave.*

JO. —if I disturbed you, I'm sorry—

LAURIE. I only ducked in here to—to. You know.

JO. Escape?

LAURIE. A fellow refugee, then.

> *Pause.*

JO. Don't go away.
—Unless you'd rather.

> *Neither of them is sure what to do.*

LAURIE. I think I've had the pleasure of seeing you before, madame.

JO. I believe you live next door. "Sirrah."

> *They both almost laugh a little.*

LAURIE. Funny how stiff one gets in these situations. Drag me to a social and I'm a cat on a leash.

JO. *(Points to herself.)* Dead cat on a leash.

LAURIE. How is your little sister, Miss March?

JO. She's fine, Mr. Laurence. But I'm not "Miss March."—I'm Jo.

> *She sticks out her hand in a businesslike manner. Laurie, taken aback, takes it.*

LAURIE. I'm not Mr. Laurence. I'm Laurie.

> *She shakes his hand with great vigor; it is a very new experience for him.*

JO. Laurie Laurence. That's terr…ific.

LAURIE. My real name is Theodore, but the boys called me Dora, so I thrashed 'em into saying Laurie instead. *(That's not true.)*

JO. *(Impressed.)* Really?

LAURIE. —No.
I've never, um, thrashed anybody. *(Trying to be impressive.)* Yet.

JO. Tell you a secret? —I hate Josephine too.
Do sit?

LAURIE. Thanks awfully. These pumps hurt like the devil.

JO. These boots are dainty little tortures—but as Aunt March says, Let Us Be Elegant Or Die.

　　　They sit.

LAURIE. …who's Aunt March?

JO. I'm a businessman—lady, I mean, so I wait on my great-aunt for wages, and she's a nasty old cat. But she's taking me to Europe in the new year! Wouldn't bring me along 'til I could pay for my own board, but I've finally saved up enough to go.
And who knows what I can become in Europe?

LAURIE. …I know something about doing the bidding of cross old people.

JO. D'you work?

LAURIE. No, I get tutored. My grandfather has great plans for me, and bought me out of the draft. I am someday to be a tedious titan of industry! So I must grind away 'til college, where I will learn how to do what I don't wish to do, in order that I may do MORE of what I don't like in the future.

JO. Lucky!

LAURIE. What?

JO. —lucky to go to college! How can you complain of that?

　　　He looks at her.

—I'm sorry, I'm being—I'm so awkward, I always talk too openly. If Meg was here she'd cough herself into a fit over me being boyish.

LAURIE. No, I… I like it.

JO. I'm not very good at being a, you know, a "lady."

LAURIE. I'm not very good at being a "gentleman."

So perhaps we should—be ourselves.

> *Pause. She's being very bad by saying this:*

JO. Do you mind if I take these boots off? They're killing me.

LAURIE. —May I do the same?

> *They're being very bad. They sit on the floor and take off their boots.*

JO. *(With great relief.)* Christopher Columbus.

> *They compare feet.*

Look at them, side by side!

> *They wiggle their toes; their feet are almost the same. Perhaps they compare sizes. A happy moment.*

LAURIE. I'd rather be a girl than a boy.

JO. You wouldn't!

LAURIE. Then I wouldn't have to do all the things that men are supposed to: waste away life in billiards and business, march off to war, be as unfeeling as granite!
If I were a lady, I'd compose on the piano all day, and nobody would bother me.

JO. Nobody would bother you except to tell you to wash the dishes, or tend the children, or catch a man before you become an old maid. At least your grandfather has plans for you! I'd like to be a—a great writer, or a famous actor, or a soldier alongside my father, but I'm scarcely let out of the house without being told what a disgrace I am! If I were a boy, people would care more about what I *could* do than what I *should* do, and I'd be thought a tremendous talent instead of a—a big ugly stone in the flower garden.

LAURIE. Not ugly at all.
(Getting suddenly shy.) I mean. I like your—gloves. They're spandy.

JO. "Spandy"!

> *She pulls out her notebook and writes in it.*

LAURIE. What's that?

JO. My notebook—I always carry it with me, to write down words for my great novel someday! "Spandy."

> *She writes it and puts it away.*

An outfit is made by gloves, that's what Marmee says.

LAURIE. Marmee?

JO. We say it instead of Mother—you must think that childish.

LAURIE. Not at all. Your ah, Marmee? I watch her, in your parlor. That is. Sometimes when you forget to draw the curtain, I can see you all together.

I haven't got a mother, you know. Anymore. So.

> *Pause.*

JO. ...That polka is gay, isn't it?

LAURIE. Do you like to dance?

JO. No. Well, yes—but I'm sure to break something or step on somebody's toes. Or step on something, or break somebody's toes.

> *He holds out his hands.*

LAURIE. I'm hardy enough.

> *She gets very shy.*

JO. Oh—I'm such an awkward old fellow, honestly.

LAURIE. Come on. *Jo.*

> *He holds out his hand.*

What are you: afraid?

JO. YOU should be afraid,—Laurie.

> *She takes it. They start, bang into each other.*

LAURIE. No, no—you lead!

> *She laughs and they galumph, laughing, until they whirl into the curtain—Jo ends up spilled on the floor. They're both laughing hysterically. As they're distracted, Meg limps through the main entrance to the little alcove—supported by Brooks.*

JO. Oh! Meg—I—

LAURIE. Brooks—we were just—

BROOKS. Theodore! WHERE are your SHOES?

> *They are naughty schoolchildren, and caught. They struggle into their shoes.*
>
> *Meg is limping, can't walk. Jo helps Meg aside; the gentlemen politely give them some privacy.*

MEG. —Jo, I can't see ANYTHING, there was a blur and then pop went my ankle—

JO. I have your glasses, do you want them?

MEG. *(Mortified.)* With the gentlemen looking?—

JO. Can you walk home?

MEG. *(Conscious of the men overhearing.)* —we can't afford a carriage.

LAURIE. Miss March, I can't bear a damsel in distress. You must take our coach!

> *Meg nods.*

Bully! I'll just bring our man around.

MEG. Give the Mingotts our regrets, Jo—

JO. "Bully"!

MEG. *(Trying to catch at Jo.)* —IN AN APPROPRIATE MANNER. *(COUGH COUGH COUGH.)*

> *Jo, excited, punches Laurie in the arm.*

LAURIE. Ow!

JO. Race!

> *They run out. Meg is having the worst night ever. She gropes about for the glasses that Jo left near her.*

BROOKS. Miss March, I must have given you a wrong turn in the dance, it's my leg—

MEG. *(Almost crying.)* No, no, I got myself into this. I was being childish—and silly and too vain about my looks and now everybody's evening is ruined.

> *He kneels by her, painfully.*

BROOKS. —nobody's evening was ruined—

MEG. *(Finds the glasses.)* Pardon me—

BROOKS. And I don't think you ever could be too vain—

> *She finally gets the glasses on, gets a good look at him.*

About your looks.

MEG. Oh!

> *Laurie and Jo race back in, both the worse for wear.*

LAURIE. *(Off.)* Cinderella, your carriage awai—

> *He stops short, almost backs out.*

oh.

JO. *(Surveying the scene, with disgust.)* …oh.

> *As they transition, Mrs. Mingott comes through, hauling along a truly horrifying man:*

MRS. MINGOTT. Miss Josephine! Miss Josephine! I've dug somebody up!

Scene 7

> *Jo dresses as the mustachioed villain Rodrigo again; they rehearse her play. Meg is dressed in lavish costume jewelry—and in some level of scandalous disarray. She's bound, struggling, to a conveniently repurposed piece of furniture, as Jo casts a spell.*

JO.

> *O my fair Lucella*
> *You shall yet be my bride*
> *My spells will hold and bind you*
> *Captive at my side!*

MEG.

> *O sad, my heart! O mad, my part! O, what end of a maiden's art!*

Jo, I have some questions about this rhyme scheme.

JO. Keep going!

MEG.

> *I loved you once, Rodrigo*
> *But those days are no more—*
> *I can't go back to being*
> *Who I was before!*
> *All things change, Rodrigo*
> *Whatever spell you say!*
> *You can't turn me to stone*
> *And you can't make me stay—*

34

JO.

> *I can make whatever thing*
> *That I wish come true!*
> *I am ALL-POWERFUL!*
> *I'll show the world—show you!*
> *I'll just take you back in time*
> *I'll turn back that clock!*
> *Back to those better days*
> *Time itself I mock!*
> *I won't accept this change*
> *Not now, and not ever—*
> *I'll make you stay the same*
> *And I'll make it last forever!*

MWA ha HA HA HA HA! MwA ha Ha ha Ha!

> *Someone's missing a cue.*

BETH. Meg:

> *She holds up the cue book for Meg to read.*

"Lucella screams thrillingly."

> *Jo makes the "go, go" sign. Meg screams thrillingly.*

AMY. —O SWEET RUBELLA!

> *Amy enters with a big flourish, dressed as a knight—complete*
> *with bad beard. She waves a gilt sword. It's the Amy show.*

THE OTHERS. LUCELLA!

AMY. This beard keeps falling off.

JO. Back!

> *Amy stomps off.*

BETH. "Lucella screams thrillingly."

> *Meg screams thrillingly.*

AMY. O SWEET LUCELLA!

> *Pause.*

Line!

BETH. "It is I—"

AMY. It is I, brave Valentino, a Wandering Knight of Some Renown!
Sword, to her dalliance—

THE OTHERS. *(Variously.)* DELIVERANCE!

AMY. …Line!

BETH. Sword to her—

AMY. *(Drops the sword, screams girlishly.)* Eek! *(Picking it up.)* Deliverance—

JO. Stop, stop—

AMY. Speed to the breast of my manly foe—!

> *She moves stylistically to stab Jo in the heart.*

JO. STOP! This isn't working.

AMY. Of course it's not working, you won't let me get my lines out!

JO. The problem here is that Amy is not a convincing gentleman—

> *Amy reacts badly.*

And if it's not realistic, why should we care?

MEG. This is a play about a wizard.

JO. But without any truth, it's dry and stakeless.

MEG. Perhaps I could play the gentleman, and Amy Lucella!

AMY. *(Excited.)* Ooh—

JO. Amy's too little.

AMY. *(Pure rage.)* OOH!

JO. I regret to inform you, Amy, that you are dismissed.

AMY. "Dismissed"?!

JO. You can't help who you are, dear. But I shall give you a nonspeaking role: a fairy, or a servant / or—

AMY. Servant!

JO. *(Snaps.)* —a woodland creature!

AMY. You cannot dismiss me—because I QUIT! This role is STUPID and this play is STUPIDER—it's for CHRISTMAS but it doesn't have anything to DO with that, no angels or nativity or Saint Nick or ANYTHING—

JO. Seasonal pageants are BORING, Amy, I am TRYING to do something ORIGINAL—

AMY. and YOU, stupid old Josephine, are absolutely—AUTOMATIC!

They all take a second trying to figure that out—

MEG. …autocratic.

AMY. RRRAAARNNNGGGH!

Amy throws down the sword and storms off.

JO. There are no small roles, Amy, only small actors!

MEG. Jo, this is supposed to be fun.

BETH. Maybe—maybe it's hard for Amy because, she, she's pretending to be someone who's so different from herself. Maybe if this play were about—real stories, about girls like us—

JO. —those stories are even more boring than seasonal pageants. No, no, the play is perfect—

MEG. Ahrm—

JO. I just need to rethink casting.

MEG. You don't mean to put Beth in?

BETH. *(Terrified.)* No—!

JO. I don't want anybody in the wrong role. I shall just SPIRIT UP an errant knight, a wand'ring gentleman—somewhere, SOMEHOW…

She wanders up to the playing space, seems to be thinking, then gets possessed, chants a "spell."

hmm hummena—humeena, HUMEENA HUMMENA SHALAKA-ZAM!

During Jo's spell—a chest has begun rocking as if possessed, scaring the wits out of Beth—and out pops Laurie, brandishing a prop sword.

MEG. Mr. Laurence!

JO. The Brave Valentino! *EN GARDE!*

LAURIE. EN GARDE!

Laurie and Jo duel boisterously—it may devolve into wrestling—with much En Gardeing and ha-HAing. Very Errol Flynn. Beth hides from the stranger.

MEG. JO! May I speak to you for a moment?

JO. Hold, Valentino—the diva wishes an aside!

Meg pulls Jo aside forcibly.

MEG. We don't want boys here, Jo! He'll make fun of us!

JO. Laurie isn't like that, Meg! We've become such friends in the last week! And he knows loads about swordfighting and mustachios and wonderful man things that I, for one, want to know!

MEG. This is a ladies' club!

LAURIE. A few of these keys are broken, aren't they? I tinker around with my own piano a bit, perhaps I could fix them?

Beth, petrified, nods. He starts fiddling with the keys.

JO. —See?!! Gentle as any girl! And he's lonely in that big house, with nobody to talk to but his mean old grandfather and that stuffy tutor Brooks.

MEG. Mr. Brooks isn't stuffy.

JO. Please, Meg, please? *(Echoing Meg's plea back to her.)* I want it—I need it, so much.

Beth hesitatingly plays a note or two; it sounds a little better.

MEG. Mr. Laurence.

She gives an elaborate actressy curtsy.

Welcome to our comp'ny.

Laurie gives an elaborate bow back. Jo jumps on him and pumps his arm up and down.

JO. Beth, strike up a victory march!

Beth shyly starts playing.

LAURIE. I'll find a way to fix those keys—

Amy stomps back on; she's been crying.

AMY. You MUST allow me to do Valentino, I've finally got it to stick—oh. My. God.

She sees Laurie, is mortified.

LAURIE. The damsel! *(He may bow.)*

Amy feels her beard, looks at her boyish outfit, squeals in despair, and runs off. Beth almost goes after her.

JO. Play, Beth! PLAY!

Hannah has entered.

HANNAH. Ladies—

JO. EN GARDE!

> *Beth plays a victory song. Jo and Laurie roughhouse.*

LAURIE. EN GARDE!

HANNAH. LADIES!

> *Mr. Laurence, an imposing old gentleman with a cane, has entered.*

A Gentleman's Come Calling.

LAURIE. Grandfather!

MR. LAURENCE. —Brooks tells me that you've been neglecting your studies, Theodore.

LAURIE. (I—)

MR. LAURENCE. You have a part to play, sir. And not amongst the women.

LAURIE. Grandfather—

MR. LAURENCE. We are too old for these games! *(Bangs cane down.)* Come!

> *Laurie leaves the stage. They begin to exit.*

JO. No—!

MEG. *(Whispered.)* Jo!

JO. *(Getting tangled up but persisting.)* You can't keep him locked away, like an ogre! He's a growing boy, he needs company and amusement, and—and sunlight in which to bloom!

MEG. *(Mortified.)* My God, Jo, what are you *saying*?

MR. LAURENCE. He doesn't need your rescue, madam, he's not some damsel in distress.

JO. He's a gentleman in distress! And without him, our play is a disaster. *Please?!!!*

> *Beth, from behind the piano, arises. Mr. Laurence notices her for the first time. He starts—then turns and exits. Laurie, unhappily, bows to Jo and follows.*

(In any other circumstance this would be the worst profanity possible.) Christopher Columbus.

MEG. Jo, you shouldn't have interfered.

JO. I can't abide seeing a body stuffed into the wrong role.

HANNAH. Oh, I don't know, Miss Meg—it's good to make friends with that boy. He may take a shine to one of you.

MEG. Hannah!

HANNAH. Ho-ho!

She exits.

JO. *(Kicks a prop.)* This is all that abominable Brooks' fault, for tattling!

MEG. He isn't abominable!

JO. What?

Amy has entered, dressed to the gills.

MEG. YOU'RE abominable!

JO. What??!

Meg storms off.

Actresses. *(Looks at Amy.)* Why are you all dressed up?

AMY. Where is Laurie?

JO. Gone.

AMY. This is all your fault, Josephine! You have RUINED my day, and Meg's day, and—and CHRISTMAS!

She also runs off. Jo, looking for consolation, turns to Beth—who slips out.

Scene 8

The Laurences' fine house. Mr. Laurence reads. Offstage, Laurie takes a Latin lesson from Brooks. As their voices fade, a light knock on the door.

MR. LAURENCE. Enter.

No answer.

ENTER!

He bangs his cane once firmly. The door creaks open, slowly. Beth, very afraid—trembling—stands on the threshold. Mr.

Laurence sees her and starts up—he seems quite struck by her.
He bows. A moment of silence.

Madame.

> *Pause. Beth is ready to flee. Beth opens her mouth to speak, but*
> *no sound comes out.*

BETH. *(A completely inaudible whisper; all the audience will see is her*
lips moving.) —Mr. Laurence—

MR. LAURENCE. I can't hear you, madame—

BETH. *(Barely a whisper, now almost in tears.)* Mr. Laurence, sir I
came to ask you—

MR. LAURENCE. Speak up—

BETH. *(Summoning up all her courage.)* Mr. Laurence, sir I came
to ask you—if you won't let, please, your grandson do our—our
theatrical.

> *Beat. She's ready to bolt at any moment.*

MR. LAURENCE. Why do you girls all think Theodore needs
rescuing? Am I—as your sister said, an ogre?

BETH. N—no, sir. Lonely.

MR. LAURENCE. Me!

BETH. Laurie, sir. And he was kind about my piano, and looked so
happy when Meg said he might join our comp'ny. And if not—our—
our play is a disaster, said Jo, and Amy said our—our Christmas
is—ruined.

MR. LAURENCE. What is your name?

BETH. B—Beth.

MR. LAURENCE. You must think me the villain from Mr. Dickens'
book, Beth March, to ruin Christmas.

BETH. I—I think people don't always see exactly what they do, sir.

> *Beat.*

MR. LAURENCE. I imagine you see.
I had a little girl once, with eyes like yours.

> *He looks at her. She looks away, embarrassed, and can't help*
> *but look at the big shining piano.*

You like that piano?

She nods.

That belonged to her. Theodore's mother.

BETH. What happened to her?

MR. LAURENCE. She grew up.

She, in a great burst of courage, touches his hand. He looks at her. He clears his throat.

Run back to your mother!

Beth curtsies and flees. He struggles up, plays a few notes on the piano… as we transition to:

Scene 9

Jo is once again attempting to direct the Christmas play. Morale is much lower than last time.

MEG.
O sad, my part! O mad, my heart! O, what end of a maiden's art!

JO. *(No patience.)* OTHER WAY. "O sad, my HEART! O mad, my PART!"

MEG. *(No patience.)* No notes, Jo! You're lucky we came back at all!

AMY. *(Popping her head out angrily.)* YES, NO notes, Josephine, you promised!

Jo turns to Beth. She nods. Jo, very irritated, gives the motion to proceed.

MEG. *(Pointedly.)* "O sad, my HEART! O mad my PART—"

LAURIE. *(Off.)* "O WHAT ENNNNNNNND TO A MAIDEN'S ARRRRRRRT???!!!"

Laurie enters with a big theatrical flourish. General mayhem.

JO. Brave Valentino!

LAURIE. The foul Rodrigo!

> *They embrace manfully—then Jo punches him in a joyful, comradely fashion.*

Ow!

> *Amy has frantically torn off her beard.*

MEG. What are you doing here?

LAURIE. *(Dancing Meg around.)* It's a holiday miracle, Lucella!— may I rejoin your comp'ny?

MEG. No—

JO. MEG!

MEG. No, Laurie, not if it upsets your grandfather!

LAURIE. It's blessed by the old man himself! He had a visitation of the conscience.

> *He turns and looks at Beth, who is overwhelmed.*

JO. Beth?

AMY. She couldn't have!
She's—she's—Beth!

> *Beth turns and leaves the room.*

JO. *(Coming out of her shock.)* What—what can I ever do for her? What can I—anything! Christmas! What does she want for Christmas?

AMY. What is she buying herself with her dollar?

MEG. She's buying something for Marmee.

JO. I never felt like such a selfish child. I'll do the same: I'll buy Marmee something, instead of a gift for myself.

MEG. Me too.

> *They look at Amy; she tries hard to look anywhere but at them.*

AMY. —

—

— — — — — — — — —

All *right*! I will, too.

MEG. That's all that Beth wants, I'm sure.

> *Laurie may sit at Beth's broken little piano, begins playing*

43

"Hark! The Herald Angels Sing"—the broken keys are especially obvious.

LAURIE. —we can do better than that.

He may play as we transition into:

Scene 10

Christmas morning. The Marches' parlor is decorated festively—wreaths and flowers and mistletoe. A basket sits on the breakfast table. The girls lead Marmee in, blindfolded. They position her:

JO. Three... two...

They take off Marmee's blindfold.

ALL GIRLS. MERRY CHRISTMAS!

MEG. —It's all for you, Marmee!

JO. Army shoes, best to be had!

BETH. Handkerchiefs—

JO. Beth did the embroidery!

AMY. And cologne, that's from me!

MARMEE. Girls—how?

AMY. We all spent our dollars!

MARMEE. You shouldn't have.

MEG. We had a visitation of the conscience.

She pokes Beth.

MARMEE. What about your gifts?

BETH. —we have enough.

They all bask in their happiness for a moment.

MARMEE. You're all growing up so fast.

BETH. Look at the flowers, Marmee—and we hung up mistletoe, you see—

Beth shows Marmee the Christmas trappings.

44

JO. *(Bad play-acting.)* Beth. What is that over there?

> *They're all very excited.*

BETH. What?

MEG. In the corner.

JO. Maybe Saint Nicholas came.

AMY. *(Delighted to be in on the joke.)* Yes, it must have been Saint Nicholas!

JO. Go and look.

> *Beth, confused, goes and slips off the blanket in the corner—uncovering a beautiful new cabinet piano.*

MEG, AMY, and JO. MERRY CHRISTMAS!

JO. Good strong oak—no broken keys here—

MEG. See the brackets, to hold candles—

AMY. And look, real silk—

MARMEE. Girls—*how?*

JO. Not us, Marmee—

MEG. Look at the card.

> *Beth, overwhelmed, opens the card—cannot read it. Marmee looks over her shoulder.*

MARMEE. "To the ghost of Christmas Past—from Mr. Scrooge."

> *Beth hesitantly runs her fingers over the keys; plays a few notes of "Battle Hymn"—stops, backs away—*

Beth?

> *—and runs right out the front door.*

JO. Beth!   MEG. —Beth!

> *Amy runs to the window as Jo runs after Beth—*

AMY. She's running to the   MARMEE. Fetch her coat, she'll
Laurences'!—   catch her death—

> *They open the door to rush after her and Jo.*

Oh, she's coming out again—   MEG. She can't handle so much
                                                       excitement—

> *Meg hurtles back inside—*

MEG. *(Panicked.)* here they come!!!

AMY. —here they ALL come!

> *Amy primps fast as Laurie and Jo burst in. Meg is also primping fast, looking towards the door—*

JO. Hurrah, Huzzah, Hail the conquering heroes!

LAURIE. EN GARDE!

JO. EN GARDE!

> *They roughhouse with much grunting and fighting—perhaps Laurie ends with a big "DIE, VILLAIN" with much splurting of fake blood—then he realizes that he's standing in front of Marmee.*

LAURIE. Mrs. March—pardon me, I—

MARMEE. *(Sticking out her hand for a friendly handshake.)* Please.— *(Pressing his hand.)* call me Marmee.

> *Beth enters with Mr. Laurence. Brooks trails after. Beth begins to play "The Battle Hymn."—They all gather around under the photograph, which seems to glow—time may slide just a little bit—and:*

Scene 11

> *Beth now transitions to "Joy to the World" slowly, as if she's been playing for some time.*

MARMEE. Beth, you'll wear yourself out.

> *Beth, smiling, shakes her head and keeps playing. Marmee returns to the table.*

I think she'll never stop.

BETH. I wish I never had to.

JO. Your fingers are going to fall off!

> *Beth plays with one hand while wiggling the fingers on the other. Brooks, who has been hanging back, suddenly crosses the room to the opposite side, where Meg is talking to Jo.*

46

BROOKS. Miss March.

> *He stares at Meg for a moment.*

Merry Christmas.

MEG. Oh. Um. Merry Chr—

BROOKS. Would you—would you like to dance?

JO. Oh my God.

MEG. ...Now?

BROOKS. There's music.

JO. CHRISTMAS music, Brooks.

BROOKS. *(Still holding his hand out to Meg.)* I'd like to try again.

JO. Oh my God!

BROOKS. —I'm sorry, you're—it's—I'll (go)—

MEG. No! I mean yes. Yes. Let's.

JO. Oh my God.

> *Meg gives her a look. They slowly, politely dance to the music. It's desperately awkward.*

AMY. D'AWWWW!

MARMEE. Amy! Hush.

> *Laurie crosses to Jo.*

LAURIE. You see that?

JO. No, Laurie, I went blind for the holidays.

LAURIE. It's romantic!

JO. It's disgusting!

LAURIE. Do you have such a low opinion of matrimony?

JO. Matrimony?! This is one dance. One incredibly awkward dance.

LAURIE. That's how it starts...

JO. Meg is too young to be thinking about marriage.

LAURIE. We all grow up, eventually...

> *He sneaks his fingers up her arm.*

JO. Stop! How could Meg want—that?

LAURIE. *Desgustibus / non est desputadum,*

BROOKS. *(Getting nearer and correcting his pronunciation.)* Desgustibus non est desputadum.

> *Brooks and Meg move away.*

LAURIE. —whatever Brooks said—taste is not disputable.

JO. He *would* lecture in a dead language. Stuffy old Brooks!

LAURIE. What do *you* want, old fellow? *(Covering a little.)* For Christmas.

JO. Boot lacings.

LAURIE. Be serious. What do you really want, Jo, more than anything? I'll buy it for you.

JO. Genius. Don't you wish you could buy it, Laurie?

LAURIE. I wish a great many things.

> *He clears his throat and holds out his hands.*

Well?

JO. Well what?

> *Jo gives him a look like he's proposed setting herself on fire. Laurie still holds out his hands.*

LAURIE. I thought you liked to dance?

JO. Not like that.

LAURIE. —we can take off our shoes—

> *Amy has been sneaking up and eavesdropping.*

AMY. I'll dance with you, Laurie!

> *Jo makes the "go ahead" gesture.*

LAURIE. I'll get you yet, Jo…

> *He turns and bows to Amy. He leads her to the only other cleared space on the carpet. Amy carefully positions herself.*

AMY. Laurie. Look.

> *She points above his head.*

Mistletoe.

> *He shrugs and leans in to kiss her cheek; she leans WAY in and grabs his head to go for the mouth—*
> *And there's a knock on the door.*

48

MARMEE. Who could that be?

AMY. Do we have to get it RIGHT NOW?

Laurie is pulling away to see—

LAURIE. Perhaps it's Saint Nicholas!

AMY. BETH, KEEP PLAYING. Laurie?!!!!!

Beth, who had faltered a little bit, keeps going; Marmee opens the door...and there's a messenger. Please note that this messenger MUST NOT be in a military uniform.

MESSENGER. Is this the March household.

MARMEE. It is.

MESSENGER. Telegram.

Beth stops playing. The messenger turns to leave.

MARMEE. *(Calls after her.)* Merry Christmas!

She exits wordlessly. Marmee opens it, reads, and sits heavily.

JO. Marmee?

MARMEE. "Mrs. March:
Your husband is gravely wounded. Come at once.
Harewood Hospital, Washington."

AMY. *(Very small.)* but it's—it's Christmas.

Marmee puts a hand over her eyes, which really scares the girls.

MR. LAURENCE. We'll get you a ticket to Washington, Mrs. March—next train out.

LAURIE. I'll run to the station now.

MARMEE. Oh—but it's Christmas, you (must have)—

LAURIE. So let me give you something—Marmee.

Marmee nods. He races off.

BROOKS. *(Suddenly, awkwardly.)* Mrs. March! Let me go with you.

MARMEE. Oh, no—

BROOKS. A lady shouldn't be down there unescorted. Let me do my duty.

He salutes. She nods. Mr. Laurence exits; Brooks escorts him, shaking his hand at the door.

49

MARMEE. Jo—I'll need what we have in the kitty.

Jo, still in shock, is looking at Brooks.

AMY. If we empty the kitty, how will we pay the rent?

MARMEE. Shh, Amy, I don't know.
Jo? I'm going to need...all of it.

Jo looks at her.

I don't think you can go to Europe, dearest. Not this year.

Jo looks at her, backs away.

Jo?

And runs out the front door.

MEG. Jo!

*Marmee begins grabbing things here and there to pack—
she's not thinking very clearly. Amy follows her as she does.*

AMY. But—we've been good and worked so hard, and gave up
presents—and now we can't have the theatrical or do anything
and—it's not fair.

MARMEE. I know.

Beth and Marmee and Amy exit.

MEG. Mr. Brooks.—I hope that— *(Starts to cry.)* our father will be
better soon, and you—

BROOKS. Miss March, please don't cry.

MEG. —and you may be back about your business quickly—I'm
sorry—

BROOKS. I mean—you *may* cry, if you like, I just—

MEG. It's just, my papa—

BROOKS. I would do anything to. To help you. You do know that,
Miss March?

MEG. Call me Meg.

*She gives him her hand. He kisses it, then presses it to his hot
cheek. She stands still.
Amy comes back in, stops short. Beth, behind her, runs into
her. They look at each other, little girls—back out, back into
their mother.*

Marmee sees the scene, clears her throat. Meg and Brooks separate immediately. Brooks bows and leaves.

MARMEE. Come round me, girls.

Meg, Beth, and Amy all gather around her to say goodbye.

Where is Jo—

JO. *(Bouncing in the front door.)* HEEERE I AMMMMM!

Jo slings a big wad of money down.

And here's to bringing Father home!

MARMEE. You haven't done anything rash?

JO. I only sold what was my own.

She takes off her hat—all of her hair is cut off.

AMY. Jo! Your one beauty!

JO. *(Very fast.)* I was wild thinking of Father, and us not being able to make the rent, or, or—do anything—and you always say we each can play our part—and I thought of the wigmaker's shop, and how I always see tails of hair there. And so I ran down the street and pounded on the wigmaker's door and burst into his Christmas and scared his wife half to death, but their son is in the army, so once I blubbered it all out she made him give me a good price—twenty-five, see?!!! I never felt a thing, just a big weight off my shoulders. And I saved a lock for you, so you could lay it away, as you did when we were children. I bet it's the last girl's lock you'll ever have from any of us—from, from me.
(Anxiously.) Marmee—aren't you pleased?

Marmee is ready to cry. She will never have a little girl again. She takes the lock; holds on to Jo—, looks at them all. Clears her throat.

MARMEE. My little women.

She hugs them one last time and prepares to go. They begin to march about in a circle, as they did when going off to work.

Marches, March!

They march bravely as they did in the beginning, singing as Marmee leaves—

MARCH GIRLS.

> *Sisters sisters will you join us!*
> *Sisters sisters will you join us!*
> *Sisters sisters will you join us!*
> *For the Union keeps us strong!*

>> *The song sags and falls flat as the girls fall one by one. They sit about the old stage with Christmas decorations. Marmee is away.*

Scene 12

AMY. It feels as if there's been an earthshake.

JO. "Earthshake"!

> *Jo takes out her little book—takes out a pencil with a big excited flourish.*

MEG. Earth*quake*, Amy.

AMY. Don't write that down, Josephine. Don't you dare write that down!

> *Jo looks at her—writes it down.*

JOSEPHINE!

MEG. *(Shouting.)* Amy, don't shout, it isn't ladylike!

AMY. Tell her not to write!

JO. Tell her not to put on airs!

BETH. My head hurts.

HANNAH. *(From the kitchen.)* Girls, STOP YELLING! *(Very loud.)* YELLING IS NOT FOR LADIES!

GIRLS. YES HANNAH

HANNAH. And if you don't clean up that mess, I'll give all your things to the street Irish, I swear I will!

GIRLS. YES HANNAH

JO. We really ought to pull these decorations down.

> *They don't do anything.*

BETH. *(Rousing herself.)* I can't, for I'm going to visit the poor

52

Hummel children—the baby's been sick. You or Meg ought to go with me, Jo—I don't know what to do for her.

MEG. I can't today, Beth—I have to write to Marmee.

AMY. And to Brooooooooks—

MEG. Don't be impertinent, Amy—

JO. Don't be RIDICULOUS, Amy—

MEG. AND I have to dictate the week's menu to Hannah, for I'm mistress of the house now, you know.

HANNAH. *(From the kitchen.)* OH REALLY, MISS MEG? YOU OUGHT TO LEARN TO COOK YOURSELF, HEAVEN KNOWS YOU'RE OLD ENOUGH

JO. "Mistress of the house."

HANNAH. "DICTATE THE MENU" MY LEFT FOOT *(Indignant banging of pots.)*

BETH. Jo?

JO. I can't today—I have business.

AMY. What *business*?

　　　Jo shrugs.

(Jealously.) Plans with Laurie! He was whispering to you yesterday— I know you're plotting something!

JO. Eavesdropping is *very* Un*lady*like.

　　　Amy is enraged.

BETH. Will you come with me to the Hummels, Amy?

AMY. I cannot go to see the dirty little Hummels, Elizabeth! For I have business of my own! Big, IMPORTANT business!

　　　The door opens.

LAURIE. *(Sticking his head in.)* Hallo! …Why all the long faces??

JO. *(Stopping him in a deliberately melodramatic fashion, staring at Amy.)* Hsst, Valentino! The WALLS have EARS.

　　　She punches him.

LAURIE. Ow!

JO. Race!

　　　Laurie races out with Jo.

HANNAH. *(Kitchen.)* MISS MEG! TIME TO GET THOSE FINE HANDS DIRTY!

> *Meg, having dug her own grave, goes.*

BETH. Amy—

AMY. *(Pulling on her coat.)* I. Have. Business.

> *She runs after Laurie and Jo.*
> *Meg yelps from the kitchen. A huge bang of pots and pans. Beth, left alone, slips on her coat to go visit the Hummels— she's dizzy and her head hurts, but she leaves the house as we transition to:*

Scene 13

> *Jo and Laurie are walking back to the house, in high celebration.*

LAURIE. Jo March, published author!

> *He throws his hat in the air.*

Huzzah! Huzzah! Huzz—

JO. —One teeny-tiny story, in one little newspaper. But my first check as a writer—thirty whole dollars, can you believe it?!

LAURIE. He ought to have paid more!

JO. You drove a hard bargain. He didn't want to give even that.

LAURIE. This is the first of many!

JO. Do you really think so?

LAURIE. You'll be the talk of the Union—of the whole planet!

JO. —I do want to be, Laurie! *That's* what I wish more than anything! I don't want to just, you know, write sentimental little ladies' stories. I don't want to have a small, well-behaved life! I want to be one of the greats, and shake the world, and outlive my time. …that must sound so childish.

LAURIE. I want you to get…everything, Jo. Everything you've ever wanted.

They've arrived at the house.

JO. I can't thank you enough, Laurie, for having the idea to do this.

LAURIE. I had to make up for you missing out on Europe, didn't I?

JO. With wages like this— *(Waves the check.)* I'll get there soon!

LAURIE. We make a good team, pulling together.

JO. A mismatched team! I don't think that publisher believed you were my agent. You ought to have said you were my brother.

LAURIE. Your brother! …No.

> *He may lean in. She looks at him for a split second, then punches him in the arm.*

Ow!

> *She enters the house.*

JO. Hallooooo?!

> *Laurie trails after her—as there is a sound from the closet. Laurie goes over, pulls open the door. Beth sits there holding a bottle of medicine and a spoon. She's been crying.*

Beth?

BETH. —the Hummel baby died, Jo. I was holding her, and I looked down, and…

I thought maybe if I prayed, or sang to her, or pretended it didn't happen, it wouldn't be true—but I was being—childish, to think I could make it better by wishing.

> *Jo moves to comfort her. Beth holds out a hand to stop Laurie from approaching.*

(Trying to be calm.) Laurie, have you had scarlet fever? Jo did, before I was born.

LAURIE. When I was seven—

JO. Scarlet fever?

BETH. The other Hummels have sore throats.
And my head hurts.

> *Amy bangs in the front door, panting—having finally caught up with Laurie and Jo.*

AMY. Aha! I'VE CAUGHT you BOTH!

BETH. *(Looking meaningfully at Laurie.)* Amy's never had it.

AMY. The GIG, I tell you, is UP!

JO. Amy, you have to go.

AMY. What?!!

JO. Laurie.

> *He begins to escort Amy out—Jo scoops up Beth.*

Scene 14

AMY. Please don't send me away!

> *Hannah stands at the center of everything, pouring out spoonfuls of medicine. Beth tosses and turns with fever in bed. Meg enters and helps to nurse Beth, as does Jo. Laurie watches all of this, helpless. Time and place run together, affected by Beth's fever dream.*

HANNAH. She'll be better in a day or two. But we'll send for the doctor, just in case.

> *She pours medicine.*

> *The doctor comes, bends over Beth. He grabs Jo's publishing money out of her hand and leaves. Beth tosses with fever. It may be flashes of things gone wrong—as if we're seeing Beth's confusion—music is minor key—everything's gone sick—*

MEG. Should we write to Marmee?

HANNAH. And frighten the poor woman?

> *The doctor comes in again, bends over Beth.*

Don't you dare. I wouldn't write to her unless it were very bad. Miss Beth will be better when the week is through.

> *The doctor shakes his head. Hannah is frightened.*

Better by next week, I'm sure.

> *Jo leaves the sick bed with rags. She is exhausted. Laurie stops her.*

JO. Laurie! You're still here.

LAURIE. Of course.

> *Jo nods—then starts, against her will, to cry.*

Please let me do something for you, Jo. You know I can't abide a damsel in distress.

JO. Laurie.

> *She looks offstage, then whispers something in his ear. Then, at normal volume:*

—Race.

Scene 15

> *Beth is in bed. Hannah replaces wet rags on Beth's face.*

HANNAH. Took care of all of you since you were babies. Each one of you growing different than the other.
Miss Beth was always so delicate.

JO. She'll be better soon, won't she?

> *Hannah does not respond.*

MEG. Hannah?—should we write to Marmee?

HANNAH. No.
I'll do it myself.

> *She rises. The girls absorb what that means as she leaves. Meg leans over Beth's bed. Amy creeps in, out of breath.*

AMY. Please don't scold me.

JO. Amy, you're supposed to be at Aunt March's.

AMY. I ran away. Please don't make me go!

> *Meg and Jo look at each other.*

MEG. Beth isn't infectious anymore.

JO. She's too young!

MEG. We're all too young for this.

> *She holds a hand out to Amy. Beth makes a little sound.*

JO. Beth!

MEG. We're here—

AMY. All of us.

BETH. Jo—tell me a story.

JO. Now?

Beth nods weakly.

BETH. A real one.

JO. Once upon a time, there was a family. A father, a mother—and four girls. But the best of them all, the conscience of the family—her name was Beth.

BETH. And when that girl died...

JO. In this story, Beth, the girl never dies.
She stayed with that family. And together, they were whole.

MEG. And together, they were safe.

AMY. And together they lived happily ever after.

JO. They *lived.*
...Beth?

Beth's eyes have closed again. Lights fade.

Scene 16

The next day, the parlor. Amy sits with her head in her hands, exhausted. She's been crying, hard. The door's bell rings—it is Laurie, sneaking in.

AMY. Laurie! *(Calling off.)* Meg, Jo! *(To Laurie.)* Where have you been?

Jo and Meg have entered.

JO. Laurie—!

He opens the door—and hands in Marmee.

MEG. Marmee—!

A frozen, tense moment as she looks for news—

JO. The fever broke, Marmee! Beth is so much better!

Marmee grabs Jo's hands, almost cries. They support her to the couch, surround her. She raises her head.

MARMEE. Merry Christmas, girls.

We have brought you—a very late present.

> *Mr. Brooks has entered, supporting a man in uniform: Robert March. He's on crutches, a bandage around his head. The girls all freeze, looking at him. Amy runs to him first, a little girl again.*

AMY. Papa!!!!

> *They all run to him, so much crying and hugging—saying "Father, Papa!"* * *Hannah enters, and freaks out. The girls are all in hysterics of joy. Jo goes to Laurie; Meg, to Mr. Brooks.*

HANNAH. MR. MARCH! *(Sobbing in joy.)* Mrs. March!

> *She accosts Marmee.*

How fast can those newfangled telegrams go, I just wrote to you this morning—!

MARMEE. Laurie fetched us yesterday, Hannah.

HANNAH. Mr. Theodore, I ought to have you whipped

> *She pulls Laurie to her bosom and smothers him.*

OH MR. MARCH TO HAVE YOU HOME AGAIN!

> *Laurie frees himself as she sobs and collapses on Mr. March.*

JO. *(To Laurie.)* Old fellow, how can I ever thank you?

MEG. Mr. Brooks—how can I ever thank you?

BROOKS. —call me John.

> *Meg takes his hand—now she presses it to her cheek. He sinks down to his knee.*

JO. Laurie—do something!—Mr. Brooks is behaving dreadfully, and Meg likes it!

LAURIE. You haven't taken any of the decorations down yet?

JO. What shall we do?

LAURIE. Jo! Look!

> *Above Laurie and Jo, the mistletoe. He kisses her. Amy looks*

---

* See overlapping dialogue at end of script.

> *over, sees them, and* screams. *Marmee bounds over to try to*
> *stop her.*

MARMEE. Shh, Amy, SHH!

HANNAH. Don't wake—

> *Too late. In the doorway, in her white nightgown, stands Beth,*
> *like a ghost. She is weak, starts on a few tottering steps—and*
> *then flies into her father's arms.*
>
> *Blackout.*

End of Act One

ACT TWO

If your production does not have an intermission, there should be a brief frozen moment, in stasis, like memory—and then we see the passage of time. Perhaps the clock's hands turn as the photograph glows. Perhaps little moments from the past scenes are acted out again and again as music plays—perhaps we see Meg leave, or even swell with pregnancy, and bounce two twin babies. Amy's hair is put up. Jo changes into a masculine outfit—and Beth observes it all. Approximately 18 months later: late summer/early fall, 1863.

Scene 1

Marmee enters with Robert. She helps him across the stage—maybe even up stairs. He's still on crutches. It's slow, slow, painful progress. He snaps the crutch back from Marmee as she tries to help him—she compresses her lips and persists. Caretaking is difficult; it costs something.

Jo watches them pass from the same makeshift stage, dustier and more worn now. Jo plays Rodrigo. Jo is now in a masculine outfit—not a dress—that she keeps on for the rest of the play. Beth watches her, sitting in the corner. She's a little graver than before. As Jo watches her parents, she tries to cast a spell over—tries to undo, tries to fix, to save.

JO.
> *I can make whatever thing*
> *that I wish come true.*
> *I am All-powerful!*
> *I'll show the world—show you.*
> *I'll just take you back in time!*
> *I'll turn back that clock!*
> *Back to those better days*

Time itself I mock!

> *Laurie enters; he's grown, too. He has friends, popularity, he's broadening into a young man—and he looks it. He has the bad gilt sword again. They fight.*

I won't accept this change
not now, and not ever—
I'll make you stay the same
and I'll make it last forever!
(*Desperately.*) MWAha ha ha HA! Mwa-ha-ha-ha—

LAURIE. Jo. Wait. Stop.

> *She lunges at him.*

Stop! What is Valentino's motivation in this scene?

JO. —What?

LAURIE. We don't have a Lucella anymore. So why does he want to fight Rodrigo? Why wouldn't they just, I don't know, go play billiards? Why are we pretending it's the same?

JO. Laurie—

LAURIE. —Now that Meg's gone, perhaps you could play the lady.

JO. Meg's coming back, she's just busy with the babies for a bit.

LAURIE. That won't change any time soon, Jo.

JO. …I'm Rodrigo.

> *She assumes the "en garde" pose. Laurie won't engage.*

LAURIE. —I need a break.

JO. Beth, five minutes?

> *Beth looks at them and leaves.*

LAURIE. Why don't you want to play Lucella? She gets to drag around in costume jewelry and scream thrillingly.

JO. (*Dryly.*) —You've answered your own question.

LAURIE. (*Comes closer to her.*) And you'd get to flirt with the loyal-hearted Valentino.

> *Jo looks at him. Pause.*

JO. Marmee doesn't approve of flirts.

LAURIE. *(Trying to be sophisticated.)* Flirting is just a game men and women play. You like games!

JO. Not that kind.

> *Pause. He tries another tack.*

LAURIE. *(Readjusting.)* —well—I'm glad! Some of the ladies I meet go on at such a rate that I'm embarrassed for them. Like Sally Mingott, if you had heard how she spoke to me at last week's dance! And if she knew how us men talked about her afterwards…huh. If you could be in my place, you'd see things that would astonish you.

JO. If I could be in your place—

LAURIE. What?

JO. Why should you mock girls for doing just what you all do? *(Very angry.)* Ladies can never win that game, can they?

LAURIE. Don't be thorny, Jo—

JO. But one set of rules for you, and another for me, isn't that right? Always! Always, always!

LAURIE. I only meant, SOME girls do flirt with me, you know, in life. But I prefer what you do! Don't do. I prefer *you*, old fellow. Just as you are.

> *Beat.*

Won't you—show me some—kindness, Jo. I'm off to college tomorrow, and won't see you for months and months.

JO. I know.

LAURIE. Will you cry, watching me ride away on my white steed?

JO. I'll be burning up with jealousy, wishing I could play your role. *(Bitterly.)* But I might as well wish for the moon. Instead, I'll wither away in Aunt March's service, clinging to her phantom promises of Europe 'til I turn gray.

LAURIE. Tell me what I can do—to make you happy?

JO. Just do your best at school. Since I can't.

> *She's close to crying.*

LAURIE. —I'll make something of myself, for you.
But promise me something in return.
Promise that you won't just mope around, snuffling. *(Jo does indeed*

sniff and stop crying.) Promise me that you'll finally finish that novel you've been scribbling away at for years, and send it out in the world.

JO. —oh, Laurie, I don't know if it's ready to go in the world—

LAURIE. We'll both get what we wish for, if we only try.
And if you send out that whopping novel—I'll give you what you've always wanted.

JO. Boot lacings.

LAURIE. Jo… I will take you to Europe.

JO. Laurie!

LAURIE. We'll go together! If Aunt March doesn't take you first…

JO. Really?!!!

LAURIE. I have the money! We'll have an adventure, you and me—just as long as we stay true to each other.
Do you promise?

> *She holds out her hand to shake. He takes it.*

JO. Go and make yourself useful out there, since you are now grown too tall to be ornamental!

> *He still has her hand. She shakes it; he doesn't let go.*

I will miss you so much.

> *He leans in. She, in a desperate attempt to be comradely, punches his arm.*

LAURIE. Damn it, Jo! We're too old for that anymore!

> *Amy careens in, panting—Beth on her heels.*

AMY. Laurie! Beth said that you need a Lucella?! *(Trying to smooth her hair and look pretty, despite being winded.)* I'll play with you.

LAURIE. We're done.

> *He looks at Jo. Amy watches them jealously.*

For now.
Swear you'll see me off tomorrow, Jo?

JO. As I am a gentleman.

> *She bows. He mock-salutes Jo, bows to the rest, and leaves, humming the "Battle Hymn"—the Marches' march song. Pause.*

Amy, we could still rehearse. You could be Lucella—*if* you promise to take it seriously, and memorize your lines properly, and—

AMY. —For whom will we be doing this play? Marmee? Father?

JO. I—

AMY. They have grandchildren to amuse them, now.

BETH. Amy—

AMY. Nobody needs this anymore, Josephine. Nobody wants it. This kind of thing is inappropriate for women of your age.
I'm doing you a favor by telling you.

She turns to leave, then:

—Did I hear you say you'll see Laurie off tomorrow?

JO. Yes.

AMY. Well, you can't. You promised to call on Aunt March with me.

JO. I spend enough time bowing and scraping to Aunt March in my working hours!

AMY. Poor people are well advised to please rich ones.

JO. So we are to waste all our days pandering to millionaires, just because they have money?

AMY. Money that we need. You pretend it's such a hardship, sitting with Aunt March, but she's paid you for it!

BETH. Amy...

JO. You have no idea what it's like! You have no idea how terrible it is to—spend years pretending to be someone you're not—

AMY. —Maybe it's time to be realistic, Josephine, about your prospects. Give up childish—and, frankly, egocentric—fantasies about Showing Them All and setting the world on fire—and you'll resent people less. It's not everyone else's fault that you don't feel like you're living up to your potential.

BETH. Amy!

AMY. Just bite your tongue and humor poor old Aunt March! You don't have to agree to be agreeable.

JO. ...what about Laurie?

AMY. He'll be better off without you.

…—Jo—tomorrow—I trust that you will wear something—appropriate.

> She leaves. Beth holds out Jo's skirt—Jo looks at it, and turns away.

BETH. Jo—

> Jo walks out. Beth looks after both of them, lost; her head hurts.

Scene 2

> Jo and Amy arrive at Aunt March's and sit. Jo is at her wits' end—but, to revenge herself, she is still wearing her masculine outfit; she may even have added the mustache back in. A clock ticks.

> Aunt March is the most gnarled, horrible woman imaginable. She has a large, nasty parrot on her shoulder. The parrot starts a scene with a great big musty SQUAWK! A tense moment as Aunt March eyes Jo's masculine outfit; Amy is mortified and angry: Maybe she tries to snatch the mustache away.

AUNT MARCH. What a…remarkable outfit, Josyphine.

JO. *(To Amy as well.)* Thank you, Aunt March. I *so* agree.

> She preens in her outfit to goad Amy; Amy would like to kill her.

AUNT MARCH. *(An order.)* Read to us.

> SQUAWK.

JO. I'm not here to work, Auntie, this is a social / (call)

AUNT MARCH. Fordyce's Sermons.

JO. Sermon One: A Lady Knows Her Place.

PARROT. Knows her place—knows her place.

AUNT MARCH. You look well, Amy.

> SQUAAAAAWK.

JO. "A lady prizes presentation."

AMY. Why, thank you, Auntie

66

Aunt March hacks something terrible up.

—so do you!

> *Aunt March vaguely examines her own phlegm as the parrot repeats:*

PARROT. So do you, so do you!

JO. "A lady speaks with discretion…"

AMY. And Polly is so charming—

> *Hungry squawk as the parrot lunges for Amy. Amy snatches her fingers back quickly.*

AUNT MARCH. Mind your fingers. *(Chuckles dryly.)*

JO. "A lady behaves cautiously"

AMY. Ahaha. Charming.

PARROT. *(Sounding like pure, happy evil.)* Charrrmiiiiing.

AUNT MARCH. How does your father fare, child?

AMY. A little better, Aunt March.

AUNT MARCH. Better! Not for long, I'm sure.

PARROT. Not for long, not for long—

JO. "A lady holds her tongue."

AUNT MARCH. He ought never to have gone to the war! But then, we should never have had a war at all.

AMY. Oh, Aunt—

AUNT MARCH. Why should we poke our noses down South? Lincoln ought never to have pressed his agenda!

AMY. Now, Auntie—

JO. "A lady holds her tongue."

AUNT MARCH. We ought to focus on the Union—and put the homeland first!

PARROT. Homeland first, homeland first!

AMY. Let's not talk politics—

AUNT MARCH. But your parents are both the same—your father and his radical abolitionism—

JO. "A LADY HOLDS HER TONGUE"

AUNT MARCH. And your mother, and her immigrant trash! I *told* her, I said, you go amongst that filthy boat rabble—

PARROT. Boat rabble, boat rabble—

AUNT MARCH. —you never know what will come trailing home after you! And look what happened! She never listened to sage advice from cooler heads, she always wished to slum around amongst the lesser classes—and so she nearly killed your half-wit sister!

PARROT. Half-wit, half-w—

> *BAM! The parrot SQUAWKS and flutters—Jo has slammed the book to the floor, or perhaps at the parrot's head—and is standing, trembling.*

AUNT MARCH. Josyphine. What on earth!

AMY. JO!

> *Jo whirls, looking at her.*

(With gritted teeth.) Just. Be. Agreeable.

AUNT MARCH. Josyphine?

> *Jo looks at Amy—and LAUGHS.*

JO. You're right! You're so right, Aunt March! You're so right, Amy! We never should have gotten into the war! Who cares if people are being enslaved? That's hundreds of miles away, why should it bother us?! Why should we take any action?!!

AMY. (Josephine—)

JO. Who cares if families are starving in the tenements?! That's right in our backyards, but why should we lift a finger?! No, no, I think we should sit on our hands and shut our mouths, lest we disturb others! Civility at all costs, that's what I say! Civility before humanity!

AMY. Jo—

JO. We should have no objections, isn't that it, Amy, no egocentric aspirations to change the world! We should be adults! And the adult thing is to do nothing and say nothing—and if we accomplish nothing, then that's for the best!

We should just stay at home, and close our eyes, and accept the SAME EVILS, FOREVER!

AMY. JOSEPHINE. You've made your point. You may be quiet now!

PARROT. *(Darkly.)* Quiet now. Quiet…nowwwww…

JO. *Christopher Columbus!*

> *Beat.*

AUNT MARCH. What a speech, Josyphine.
But I am glad to know your true thoughts, at last.

AMY. *(Attempting to undo some damage.)* Auntie—

AUNT MARCH. Miss Amy, I have long planned to make an European tour—

JO. "Long-planned" indeed—

AUNT MARCH. And since Josyphine is so cross-patched against leaving home—or keeping a civil tongue in her head—I wondered if you might like to be my lady companion?

JO. *(Starting to yell quickly.)* Aunt—Auntie, you've been promising me this for YEARS—

AUNT MARCH. DON'T YOU YELL, JOSYPHINE—

JO. AFTER ALL THIS TIME, AFTER ALL OF THIS WORK

AUNT MARCH. *(Rising over her.)* I promised to bring a lady companion! A *lady.*

PARROT. *(Darkly.)* Laaaadyyyy.

> *Beat. Jo turns to Amy.*

JO. Amy—

AMY. Yes. Yes, please, Aunt March! And thank you.

> *Jo screams in frustration. The parrot SQUAWWWWWKS.*

Scene 3

> *The Marches' parlor. Marmee rips bandages as she mediates. Jo's scream turns right into:*

JO. AAAAAAAAAAAA Marmee!

MARMEE. There's nothing to be done, Jo. Aunt chooses Amy.

JO. Amy's too young!

AMY. I'M NOT, I'm a woman grown. And it's your own fault! If you hadn't been so nasty and intemperate and bitter—

JO. Bitter—from years of swallowing bile!

MARMEE. Girls—please, you'll wake your father—

AMY. You think I'm stupid, Josephine, but I know more about the world than you ever did! You think that if you go to *Europe*, things will be so different: that you'll get to do and be whatever you want. But Europe isn't the set of one of your theatricals! You don't get to make up what happens in life! There are rules over there, just like here!

Aunt March is taking me along because I'm smart enough to keep my peace! Because I act like a lady and you never do!

JO. Don't you understand, Amy?! I would make a dreadful lady, even if I tried, even if I wanted to be one! Look, they would all say, look at that awkward boy in the dress, strangling on every thought, biting his tongue 'til it fell off! I can't ever be someone like you, so I might as well be what I am!

AMY. So be what you are, Josephine. And live with the consequences.

> *Amy exits.*

JO. It's always so. Amy gets just what she wants, and I get all the drudgery.

MARMEE. I don't think Amy always gets what she wants.

BETH. I'm glad you're not going yet, Jo—for I should miss you.

JO. I never shall go at all. I work and push and try and because I'm not exactly what people want me to be, it all gets thrown away.

MARMEE. You wouldn't enjoy the trip as Aunt March's hand-maiden, anyhow. Amy has no grand ambitions, and little else to amuse her now that she's growing up. At least you still have your writing!

JO. Marmee, I meant what I said to Amy—I never shall be a lady—I never will be a woman like you.

MARMEE. Jo—
—you don't have to be.

She exits. Beat.

BETH. Jo—

JO. I'll show Amy! I'll go to Europe, and I won't have to bow and scrape and sacrifice every part of me to get ahead! I can do it my own way!

BETH. How?

JO. My novel! I promised Laurie, and he promised me! I have to write!

BETH. Jo—

JO. I have to write!

>*Jo hurtles down, writing furiously in a red notebook. The scene transitions. The "Battle Hymn" plays as time passes.*

Scene 4

>*Months later. A knock.*

JO. I said, I have to—

>*Meg comes in—something red is on her dress. She's very tired. Jo starts up. It's all very* The Seagull.

Meg!

MEG. Hello, Jo.

>*Jo kisses her, puts down the notebook.*

JO. Meg! It's been months since you've visited!—what are you doing here?

>*Pause.*

MEG. The stage is still set up, I see.

JO. I knew you'd be back!

MEG. Am I too late for rehearsal?

>*She laughs. She's very frazzled.*

JO. Meg. Are the babies all right?

MEG. What?

JO. Is—that—is that blood?

MEG. It's—it's jam.

She suddenly bursts into noisy tears.

JO. Jam!

MEG. Blood, Jo, you've been writing too many stories! Don't be so dramatic!

She cries much harder.

JO. —why are you crying?

MEG. Where is Marmee—

JO. She's changing Papa's bandages.

MEG. I'll come back another time—

JO. You could talk to me—

MEG. I need a grown woman's perspective.

JO. I—well—I'm here, Meg.

Meg assumes a scrap of dignity.

MEG. I can't say, it's too shameful.

JO. Try.

MEG. Well—I'm home with the babies all day, you know, and Demi is starting to crawl. I can't leave him alone for a moment but I find him headed toward the fire—

JO. Yes—

MEG. And Daisy has the colic, she won't stop crying—and they're both teething—

JO. Yes—

MEG. And I never realized what an angel Hannah is here, with all the chores, they just never end—and we can't afford any help, John works hard enough just to keep a roof over our head—I'm so tired of being poor—it's not fun at all being mistress of the house, really. So I'm home alone with the twins, Jo—alone, all day. And all day of every day I'm fighting—I'm fighting a battle against all the nappies and bottles and swaddling clothes in the world, and I'm always losing.

JO. Oh, Meg—

MEG. But today—today! They finally took a nap at the same time and it was so quiet and I sat and thought, what if I could have anything I wished in the world right now? And I thought, I want—all I want—is—JAM.

She cries.

JO. *(Patting.)* It's all right to— *(Little bit lost.)* to have jam.

MEG. So I tore through our cupboards, and I found some dusty old pot of raspberry and ate it right out of the jar, Jo, like a child, and was happy for one moment. Just one little peaceful moment, just for me...

And then JUST THEN like she SENSED it Daisy woke up and started wailing and that woke Demi and HE started wailing and then I should have gone and picked them up but then I just couldn't, *I* started wailing and that's how John found me, crying and covered with jam with the babies screaming in their nursery.

JO. Oh.

MEG. And John asked why I hadn't picked up the babies and I cried and he asked why I hadn't made dinner and I cried and he asked why I was so messy and I cried—And then he told me I was being hysterical and I said hysterical is just what men call women who bear and bear what men never could, and then finally snap!

JO. Served him right! Stuffy old Brooks!

MEG. He is, isn't he? Stiff and stuffy! Thank you! And then we had a big row and I told him if he wanted a perfect lady at all times he could just go off and find one, and I stormed out.

And I just—I just wanted to come home.

Real home. You know.

JO. Of course,

MEG. —I just want to come back and be a little girl again, and not somebody's crying mother or somebody's jam-covered wife.

JO. Then DO that, Meg, come back and live here!

MEG. —Could the babies come too? I couldn't leave them.

JO. They could—they could sleep in the attic.

MEG. I don't think there'll be space enough. *(A bit like it's a nightmare.)* They keep growing and growing.

JO. Everything can be just as it was, Meg.

MEG. ...what about John?

JO. Forget him! It never happened! Stuffy old—

Brooks has entered.

Brooks.

BROOKS. Meg—I'm. I'm sorry, I've been working so hard, and I was very—cruel, very—

JO. Stiff.

BROOKS. Rigid, yes—unfeeling, very—

JO. Stuffy?

BROOKS. Very stuffy.

Please come home, Meg. I need you. The babies need you.

MEG. No.

—Not stuffy, John.

JO. Meg—

Meg puts her hand on Brooks' cheek.

MEG. Please forgive me, Jo, I was just being—childish.

JO. Didn't you want to talk to—

MEG. Jo. *I'm* the Marmee, now.

Meg and Brooks leave, hanging on to each other.

JO. O what end of a maiden's art!

She shakes it off, goes back to her book.

I have to write.

She writes in the novel. The next scene is set up behind her as she writes. The clock ticks.

Lights shift. Beth's head hurts.

BETH. Jo? You've been working so hard for months, won't you come out—and talk to me—.

Jo slams the book shut.

JO. *(Singing.)*
Glory glory Hallelujah
Glory glory Hallelujah

BETH. Jo!

JO. *(Dances around her, shrugging on a coat.)* I'm done! I'm done! If everything changes, then I'll change everything!

    Glory glory Hallelujah!
    My Truth is marching on!

       We are finished transitioning into:

Scene 5

Her red book in hand, Jo enters the publisher's office, humming—a dark, smoky den. A few gentlemen sit outside. It's pretty seedy. Jo has put on a maroon silk cravat for the occasion, carefully tied. She walks up to the publisher's door, knocks. Note: This is the first time we have ever really seen Jo out in the "real world." Jo knocks again.

MR. DASHWOOD. *(A very thick voice.)* Enter.

    Jo hesitates.

ENTER.

    Jo enters.

Whosat?

    He's a bit drunk.

JO. It's Jo. Jo March.

    She holds her hand out to shake in a businesslike fashion. He doesn't move.

MR. DASHWOOD. Who?

JO. We met last year? You published my short story in your paper? …"The Spell of Rodrigo"?

MR. DASHWOOD. I buy a lot of stories.

    Pause.

You bring another?

    He lights a cigar as she talks.

JO. —I brought something better! My very first, WORLD PRE-MIERE novel!

MR. DASHWOOD. …Novel?

JO. A whole work about Rodrigo. An epic! It has everything: love, tragedy, swordfights—pirates, mermaids, dragons, and, and death and birth, and—heavy themes. And it's set—all over Europe! So.

He picks up the book. Pause.

MR. DASHWOOD. I'm not in the market for ladies' novels.

JO. But—you have a press downstairs, with books in the window—

MR. DASHWOOD. Those are works of literature. Not sentimental pieces.

JO. This is—serious. I've worked on it for years.

As he speaks, he casually taps the novel with his cigar—getting ash on it. He eyes her outfit.

MR. DASHWOOD. I assume you're a woman?

She doesn't answer.

Then this is a ladies' novel. Doesn't matter how you dress it up.

He pokes an exploratory finger at her outfit—Jo shies away.

Listen, Miss March—there's a legitimate place for women's voices—bring me another sweet little story, it helps sell powder if I run it next to the ads.

JO. This is a whole book—

MR. DASHWOOD. Fifteen for a story. Put some heaving bosoms in it.

JO. Fifteen?
Last time you paid me thirty.

MR. DASHWOOD. Meow.

He looks her up and down.

—Seems to me that last time, you had a cooler head negotiating for you. Where's your "agent"?

Jo, humiliated, reaches for her book—he pulls it out of her reach. He may catch her hand.

76

Some gentlemen won't pay a lady at all—but I'm forward-thinking.

She can't leave without the book—it's her baby. He leers.

Miss March—a little advice: Next time you step into this world, you bring that "agent"—or your father—or your husband.

He puts his hand on her rear—matter-of-factly, almost casually—she needs the book.

Remember—I'm one of the good ones.

He gives her the book and releases her.

We transition back to the Marches' attic. Beth enters. Jo cradles her book like a baby. She tries to hold herself together. The clock ticks.

BETH. How did it go?

JO. They didn't want me—it.

She takes off the cravat—maybe crumpling it up, or very carefully folding it, as if she'll put it in a box and never wear it again.

BETH. Are you all right?

JO. I was just being—childish.

BETH. Do you want to… do you want to write? Will that make you feel better?

JO. My stories are lightweight, sentimental—they don't MEAN anything—

BETH. Oh Jo. Maybe if you tried—writing something real, something from your life—

JO. My life is—it's—nobody wants to read about that, about a house full of stupid naive little girls, about someone like me, someone awkward and deluded and not a real—a real woman, or—

BETH. That's not true—

JO. It is, and wishing it was different won't change anything!

BETH. Do you want to put on a play, or—

JO. I'm too old for all that now.

BETH. Will you tell me a story? A real—

JO. Beth. STOP.

Pause.

BETH. Can anything make you feel better, Jo?

JO. No.

> *Offstage, someone has begun whistling an old tune.*

BETH. Not anything?

> *Jo turns, elated.*

Scene 6

Approximately spring, 1864.

JO. Laurie!

> *He enters—he looks broader, much more grown up. He does a bow.*

LAURIE. Miss March—Mr. Laurence, from next door, you may remember from our misbegotten youth—

JO. Stop that!

> *She hugs him for a moment—then she pulls away and tries to punch his arm.*

LAURIE. No—!
How do I look, Jo? Like a Real College Man?

JO. You look— *(It's loaded.)* like a man.

> *He comes towards her.*

Wait— *(Steps back to look at him.)* —have you kept your promise?

LAURIE. Studied myself to a skeleton all semester, and got top marks. With honors.

JO. Oh, Laurie!

LAURIE. I was motivated.

JO. I'm so proud of you!

LAURIE. I've been a good bo—a good man?

JO. Good old fellow.

LAURIE. —How have *you* been, old fellow?

Beat.

JO. One trouble comes on top of another.

LAURIE. Come, what's the matter?

Jo doesn't answer.

—you know I can't bear a damsel in distress—!

JO. —I can't say, it's too shameful.

LAURIE. Couldn't you finish your novel?

JO. I did finish—it's right here, you see—

She holds up a red notebook on the desk.

LAURIE. Three cheers for the great authoress! Huzzah, huzz—

JO. Don't!

She slips the novel into her pocket.

I took it to the publisher and he was—dreadful, and I've been working so hard, for so long. And Amy's going to Europe because she's a lady and Meg's gone forever because she's a mother and I—I'm not anything—

LAURIE. Whoa, whoa, Jo—

JO. *(In despair.)* —there's no place for me in this world and everything's changing and everyone's growing up and away, and I don't know what to do!

LAURIE. Hold on to me.

She hugs him.

So you don't have a publisher yet—but you'll find one—or, or something!

She slowly backs away.

You've just got to keep trying!

JO. But if I don't get something published, Laurie, I'll never be one of the great minds. I'll just be a nobody, wasting my time serving old rich people like Aunt March, with no money and no importance, until the day I die and am forgotten.

LAURIE. Since when are you so grim?

JO. Since you went away.

LAURIE. Well. You don't—you don't have to make money, you know.

JO. Of course I do.

LAURIE. Perhaps someone could just…give it to you.

JO. Ha!

LAURIE. Don't laugh. A sort of a knight, maybe, like brave Valentino—

JO. —that's just a story, I should know, I'm the one who made it up—

LAURIE. A friend, then. Somebody who loves you.

> *Long pause.*

JO. Laurie—

LAURIE. —I've loved you ever since I first saw you.

> *He kneels.*

Jo…won't you?
It's perfect, you must admit that—I'm one of the family already! And I have money, so you'll never have to work again!
I told you I would take you to Europe—it'll be our honeymoon!

> *He holds out a hand. Beat.*

JO. *(Slowly.)* …So Amy is a lady, and Meg is a mother—and I'd be a wife?

LAURIE. I don't want to change you, Jo! I want you to be you, and me to be me, and us to be together.

JO. Can't we just—stay as we are?

LAURIE. I can't pretend that we're still only—little children, play-fellows. I need something more.
Don't you?

JO. …not that.

> *Pause. Laurie turns away.*

Oh, please don't cry—

LAURIE. I know it's not manful—

JO. Please, it's not that, I swear!

> *She holds his hands.*

LAURIE. Don't you love me even a little, Jo?

> *Pause.*

JO. Not a little, Laurie, so much. But not as you want me to. It's just—it's not me.

Pause. She reaches out. He shies away.
Pause. He almost laughs.

LAURIE. Well. I'm not going back to college now.

JO. What?

LAURIE. I was only there for you!

JO. Laurie, you'll get over this after a while, and find some girl who will adore you and be a lady for your fine house. Me—you'd grow ashamed of me by and by, and you'd come to hate my writing, and we would be unhappy!

LAURIE. That's not (true)—

JO. You've just built up something—in your head—you're playing a part, some idea of being a Man that you picked up from your friends or college or the world. It's *not* me—but it's not even you! We can go right back to who—what—we were. All you have to do is shake off this—childish fantasy, and—

LAURIE. —It's not childish, Jo. It's called growing up. It's real. And we can never go back.

> *She looks at him—it's as if the world has dropped away from beneath her feet. The clock only runs one way.*

…Why can't you want what any other woman would want?

JO. Because I'm not—I'm not like other women.
I thought you understood.

> *Pause. He turns to leave.*

LAURIE. I hope you get what you DO want, Jo. Whatever that is.

JO. Laurie!

> *Amy runs in, breathless—she really isn't ever cool around him. Beth arrives behind her.*

AMY. Laurie! Welcome home!!!

> *She holds out her arms for a big hug. He doesn't go for it.*

LAURIE. Not "home." Not now.

JO. Laurie—!

> *He exits.*

AMY. What was that about?

81

JO. *(Very upset.)* Nothing. Why are you so dressed up?

AMY. No reason. What did you do to Laurie?!

JO. Leave me ALONE, Amy!

> *Jo whirls away from Amy. Beth approaches her.*

BETH. Jo.

JO. I'll never get out of here, Beth. I'll never get what I need. I'm never going to Europe, or—or anywhere—

BETH. What happened?

> *Beth strokes her hair. Jo, unexpectedly, cries.*

JO. *(To Beth.)* Laurie made an offer to me—

AMY. He *what*—

JO. *(To Beth.)* And I had to refuse him—

AMY. You *what*?

JO. *(To Beth.)* I've lost my best friend, and everything's ruined forever.

BETH. Oh, Jo, nothing is forever.

AMY. How could you be so stupid?!

JO. What?!!

BETH. Amy—!

AMY. You always just do whatever you want—

JO. I NEVER get to do what I want—

AMY. —and make your own way and don't care how it affects anyone else—it's so senseless and rude and blind—

BETH. Amy!

AMY. You are—Josephine, *(The killing stroke.)* you are absolutely purist!

> *Pause. Jo almost stops crying.*

JO. Purist?

AMY. Childish! Silly!

JO. Puerile?

AMY. I—yes, fine, but *purist*, too! So—unyielding, and selfish, and Josephine, don't you dare write that down.

Jo deliberately walks over to the table, picks up another red notebook—full of Amy's malaprops, and writes it down.

Don't! I'm warning you!

JO. Why stop now. "Purist."

Jo shakes her head, almost chuckles.

AMY. You are impossible. You can't be the way you are!

JO. And yet.

She gestures to herself: What can be done.

Amy, more than frustrated, turns and stalks away.

Jo slips the book in her pocket: NOT her novel, the book full of misquotes. In order to do so, she pulls OUT the novel (also in a red cover) from her pocket, and replaces it with the notebook. She lays the novel down on the table. As this happens:

BETH. Let's go talk to Marmee.

She leans against Beth as they exit. Amy walks over to the red book and picks it up as:

Scene 7

The Laurences' house. Laurie sits playing the same sad tune he played when we first heard him. A shy knock.

LAURIE. Enter.

The door stays closed for a moment.

ENTER!

Beth steps in.

Oh.

He flings himself back down at the piano and plays a sad, sad tune. Beth slowly approaches.

BETH. Can't you play something gayer, Laurie?

LAURIE. No.

He hits a darker note.

You can tell Jo—I won't bother your family anymore.

BETH. You're family.

She sits.

LAURIE. —I'm going away, Beth.

BETH. Where?

LAURIE. Not back to college!

BETH. Maybe to Europe? *(Trying to be sneaky.)* Amy's going, you know, with Aunt March.

Laurie does not respond, hits a dark note.

I'm sure Amy would love a visit in Italy. Or a—a companion.

LAURIE. —Amy is just a little girl.

BETH. Not anymore. You must see that. And she's—she's fond of you.

Laurie hits another dark, disparaging note—does not respond. Beat.

—I came here once to talk to your grandfather, about—changing his mind—it was hard—but then things got better, for all of us.

LAURIE. Everything's ruined forever for me now.

BETH. Nothing lasts forever.

She starts to exit, then turns.

Laurie? I think—sometimes—we want so badly—we don't see what we—we have.

She exits. He stops piddling around on the piano. He plays the Marches' march: "The Battle Hymn of the Republic," one key at a time, slowly.

Scene 8

Beth reenters the parlor. Marmee is counseling Jo. Amy sits reading.

MARMEE. Escape into writing for a while, Jo. Who knows what will come of it in the end?

    She starts to leave.

I should check on Papa.

JO. Has anybody seen my book?

MARMEE. Perhaps it's under here—

    They look around the desk. Nothing. Amy reads. After a moment, Jo turns to her.

JO. Amy, do you have it?

AMY. *(Flipping her hair back.)* I…do not.

JO. *(To Marmee.)* Maybe it's in the other room—

AMY. I warned you.

JO. What?

AMY. You've been torturing me for years—writing down every word I misspoke, making me feel stupid—rampaging through life with your rough ways, never caring if you hurt Laurie or me or anybody! But you'll have nothing to show for it now, for it's gone.

    She goes back to reading.

JO. What?!

AMY. If you're looking for your notebook, Josephine— *(Gestures towards the fireplace.)* There you shall find your lesson at last.

JO. This notebook?

    She produces the notebook from her pocket.

AMY. What—?

JO. This is the book I write your malapropisms in.

MARMEE. —What did you burn, Amy?

JO. Not the—the red book here?

She gestures towards where the novel sat on the table.

(Going to the fire.) No no no no no nononono

BETH. Jo—not your novel?

> *Jo, as if she's been stabbed, has gone to the dying fire, started pawing through the ashes—*

MARMEE. Jo, no, you'll burn yourself—

> *Jo pays no attention.*

BETH. Was it her novel?

MARMEE. Amy, what have you done—

BETH. That was her only copy, Amy!

AMY. —I thought it was the notebook, they looked the same—

MARMEE. Jo, stop! Please—stop.

> *Jo finishes scrabbling through the fire, looks up—*

AMY. Josephine—

> *Jo, covered with ash, crosses very fast to Amy and SLAPS her as hard as she can.*

MARMEE. JO!

> *Beth goes to Amy, protects her—Marmee holds back Jo.*

JO. MY ONLY COPY!

MARMEE. That's no excuse for violence—

JO. YEARS of work! All my stories, my childhood—gone!

AMY. It was an accident!

JO. I can never do it again!

AMY. I didn't mean to!

JO. Jealous, you did it because you're jealous—

BETH. Jo!

AMY. I, jealous! Of an old monster like you!

MARMEE. Amy!

AMY. You great ugly boy, I shouldn't be surprised you'd treat a lady so—

MARMEE. AMY!

AMY. It serves you right!

Jo lunges at her again.

BETH. Jo, no—!

Marmee pulls Amy away, but:

AMY. I've done you a favor, Josephine, getting rid of that rubbish. Now you can FINALLY accept reality!

JO. I never shall forgive you. Never.

BETH. Jo—

JO. You and I, it's over.

> *Violence is still very much in the air; Marmee attempts to defuse.*

MARMEE. —Perhaps we should retire until dinner.

JO. I can't eat at the same table as her, Marmee.

AMY. Marmee—I don't feel safe.

JO. You shouldn't feel safe! You're not.

MARMEE. *(Looking at both of them.)* Maybe—you would like to visit Meg for a few days, dear.

AMY. Why shouldn't she go?! Why am I always sent away?!

MARMEE. *(Gesturing to the fire.)* Amy.

AMY. She always gets what she wants.

> *Jo laughs bitterly.*

But it doesn't matter. I'll go to Meg's—and soon I shall go to Europe with Aunt March. And there—there I imagine I'll meet somebody wonderful and get married, and then we never shall be under the same roof again! Me and my failure sister!

MARMEE. AMY. Let's go pack some things.

JO. You're not my sister.

MARMEE. Jo.

JO. Leave me alone.

> *Marmee leads Amy off. Jo has sunk down to the ashes again. She doesn't cry.*

BETH. Oh, Jo.

> *Jo is carefully gathering the scraps into her skirt—getting very dirty as she does.*

JO. —Amy's right.

It's been years, and we've never had peace. We're too different. We should give up, and go our separate ways.

BETH. But we're family.

JO. Why should people be forced together when they want nothing in common? Amy will go to Europe, then to some gentleman. I'll stay here—always—and get older, angrier; more and more bitter. Let us grow apart: It's healthier for everyone involved.

BETH. I can't believe that's right.

JO. People change—they move on and away. The bonds—the—the dreams—we start out with—are—childish. They don't mean anything now.

> *She finishes gathering ashes—the fire is almost completely dead.*

BETH. Jo.

JO. I'm tired of fighting—everything. Breaking myself against every wall. I'm done.

Let the war be over.

> *Jo leaves, the ashes cupped in her skirt. Beth turns—what should she do? The clock ticks. She looks up at the Civil War portrait. The ticking gets louder: nightmarish. She grabs at the mantel, weak. The ensemble may sing under; the music is going minor, wrong:*

Sisters, sisters, will you join us?
Sisters, sisters, will you join us?
Sisters, sisters, will you join us?
When the day of Judgment comes!

> *The room is whirling for Beth. Perhaps they all act out small moments from the previous scenes: repetitive movements, again and again. But it's gone demonic, wrong—conflicts, the slap, and violence and dissension and anger and divide building and building and—perhaps, distantly, battle sounds; the center will not hold—*

BETH. ...stop.

The room stops swirling—Beth falls to the floor in front of the photograph in a dead faint.

Scene 9

The song keeps going. Beth is carried to her bed and tucked in. The clock ticks. Jo sinks down by Beth's bed. A moment. The clock bongs, signaling the hour. Beth wakes up.

JO. *(Attempting to be cheerful.)* Good morning!

BETH. —was the doctor here?

JO. Marmee is talking to him now.

...how long have you been feeling sick again?

BETH. I never really felt well, after the fever. *(Testing.)* And I know—I know I'll never get better.

JO. Don't say that!

BETH. *(Hopeful.)* What did the doctor say?

JO. Hang the doctor!

BETH. So—I was right.

> *Beat. Beth attempts to process this moment; she starts to cry, but tries not to—*

JO. Please don't—please—it'll be—

> *She wants to say "all right," but can't finish the sentence.*

BETH. I'm just—I'm ashamed I've done so little.

JO. Beth—

BETH. I'm not like the rest of you. I never made plans about what I'd do when I grew up; thought of being married, or moving on—I couldn't imagine myself anything but stupid Beth, sitting at home.

JO. You're not (stupid)—

BETH. —But I never wanted to go away! I'm afraid of being home-sick, Jo.

> *Pause.*

And I worry about all of you, without me.

JO. Don't worry. I'll take care of everyone—just as you do.

BETH. What?

JO. It's all right! I've decided to give up on my fantasies about—riding out and changing the world. *(Half-rolling her eyes at herself.)* Running away to Europe. I'll stay at home, and be everything to Father and Marmee. I'll give up writing, and make the house cheerful. I'll do my duty.

BETH. What?

JO. Beth—

> She takes her hand, tenderly.

I have finally grown up.

> Beth struggles up painfully. She is VERY angry. It's pretty scary, actually.

BETH. WHAT?!

JO. Beth—!

BETH. How can you say that?!!

JO. I—I have no heart for writing anymore—and—I thought you'd be pleased!

BETH. That's not growing up! That's giving up!

JO. Please calm down?

BETH. So you'd play the new Beth to them, Jo? That's not the part for you!
You get the privilege of growing up, so use it! Don't waste your life trying to be a violet if you're—a—chestnut burr, prickly on the outside and soft inside, or a—a big rigid oak tree, or a stupid ROCK, even—or whatever you find out that you are, Jo. I don't want that!

JO. Beth. I've never seen you angry before…

BETH. You've proven you can provoke anyone.
Don't give up. Write the real stories, Jo. Write better ones.
You promise me.

> Jo nods. Beth slumps back.

JO. Is there anything I can get you, Beth?

BETH. All I want is the family I have, you bad Jo.

    Pause.

Where is Amy?

JO. Oh—she'll visit later. With Meg, and the babies.

    Beth looks at her.

BETH. I know you two are different. But make amends.

JO. I don't (think)—

BETH. Bring her, and Laurie. Bring them together.

    Pause.

Jo—tell me a story.

JO. Now?

BETH. A real one.

Scene 10

    The ensemble comes in and places flowers at the foot of Beth's bed—armfuls and armfuls, blossoms and leaves and buds and blossoms—

JO. Once upon a time, there was a family. And this family lived in a small house in the shadows of a big city. And outside the city was an even bigger country—

BETH. And that country went to war.

    Amy enters.

JO. To war with itself.

    Laurie enters.

BETH. That was hard—

    Jo takes Laurie's hand—she may even kiss his cheek. They embrace.

JO. Yes. But the family stayed together. Because even if the world had split apart: together, they were whole.

91

Jo hugs Amy as well, even if it's awkward. And then Jo consciously puts Amy's hand in Laurie's—and they stand by Beth's bedside, holding hands. Beth sinks deeper in fever.

BETH. Nothing lasts forever—

JO. And the best of them all, the conscience of the family—was named Beth.

BETH. And when that girl died...

JO. No, Beth. In this story, the girl never dies.

BETH. Marmee! Will you bring the flowers closer?

Her sisters gather the flowers and bring them to her—she relaxes, then goes further into the fever. Marmee strokes her hair; her father holds her hand. Her sisters hold the flowers out to her.

Look at them, all together.
So beautiful!

Beth closes her eyes, smiles. She is covered in flowers. Her family surrounds her. It is peaceful. A single peal of music.

JO. ...Beth?

—Beth is turned away from the audience. The ensemble sings, slowly, so quietly we may only hear some of the words (it is a funeral song):

ENSEMBLE.
Glory Glory Hallelujah
Glory Glory Hallelujah
Glory Glory Hallelujah
For the Union keeps us strong!

As Jo speaks, the scene retransitions to Jo at her desk—she tries to write.

JO. This little girl helped her family, though they were imperfect. She did her work, though it was humble. She learned her lessons, though they were small.
She didn't have magical powers. She never went on big adventures. And she loved her monster, instead of slaying it.

Beth's story wasn't a great epic.—

That's why it needs to be told.

She is now alone.

In this story, the girl never dies…

BETH. Jo.

Tell it again.

Jo puts a pen to the paper. Beth smiles.

End of Play

ADDITIONAL DIALOGUE

The following is overlapping dialogue to be used in Act One, Scenes 2 and 16. It is really under-chatter for the main dialogue, may repeat over and over again, and you absolutely need not get through all of it. My preference is that virtually none of it be heard distinctly/in the clear.

Scene 2, Page 15

MEG. JO!—what are you—get off, I mean it—get off, Jo—you are really being—this is ridiculous; Amy, grab that—oh God, Hannah is going to KILL us—Jo, I mean it. I am TELLING you, Jo, get DOWN!

AMY. JOSEPHINE! NO! Josephine, you are really ridiculous, this is way too much—Meg, stop her—she's going to knock over all of our—yuck, how can we eat any of this after her FEET have been up there—JOSEPHINE! Josephine, get down—

BETH. *(Laughing.)* Oh! Jo! You really shouldn't—Jo.

Beth can ad-lib, "Jo," as much as she wants.

Scene 2, Page 16

After Jo's line "ALL! IN! ONE!" plus Amy's scream. Only use if needed, and, again, may not need to get through all of it.

MEG. JO! Jo, OFF—Amy, calm down.

BETH. Get down now, you bad Jo.

Scene 16, Page 59

MEG. Papa! Papa, are you all right? Oh, oh, Marmee—where did you—how did you—are you all right? I can't even—I can't believe it—oh, I don't want to hurt you—Marmee, I missed you so much, we were so frightened, but she's so much better.

AMY. Papa! I missed you so much? Are you all right? I was so scared—please please let me take the bag or—what do you want, what do you need? Papa! How did you—was it the train? Did Laurie? Where did he—

JO. Papa!! Papa! Oh, sit down, Marmee, you sit too, I can't believe it—what can I get you? How did you get here—I didn't think—I never thought you would come too, I'm so happy—I can't believe it—

PROPERTY LIST
(Use this space to create props lists for your production)

SOUND EFFECTS

(Use this space to create sound effects lists for your production)

Dear reader,

Thank you for supporting playwrights by purchasing this acting edition! You may not know that Dramatists Play Service was founded, in 1936, by the Dramatists Guild and a number of prominent play agents to protect the rights and interests of playwrights. To this day, we are still a small company committed to our partnership with the Guild, and by proxy all playwrights, established and aspiring, working in the English language.

Because of our status as a small, independent publisher, we respectfully reiterate that this text may not be distributed or copied in any way, or uploaded to any file-sharing sites, including ones you might think are private. Photocopying or electronically distributing books means both DPS and the playwright are not paid for the work, and that ultimately hurts playwrights everywhere, as our profits are shared with the Guild.

We also hope you want to perform this play! Plays are wonderful to read, but even better when seen. If you are interested in performing or producing the play, please be aware that performance rights must be obtained through Dramatists Play Service. This is true for *any* public performance, even if no one is getting paid or admission is not being charged. Again, playwrights often make their sole living from performance royalties, so performing plays without paying the royalty is ultimately a loss for a real writer.

This acting edition is the **only approved text for performance**. There may be other editions of the play available for sale from other publishers, but DPS has worked closely with the playwright to ensure this published text reflects their desired text of all future productions. If you have purchased a revised edition (sometimes referred to as other types of editions, like "Broadway Edition," or "[Year] Edition"), that is the only edition you may use for performance, unless explicitly stated in writing by Dramatists Play Service.

Finally, this script cannot be changed without written permission from Dramatists Play Service. If a production intends to change the script in any way—including casting against the writer's intentions for characters, removing or changing "bad" words, or making other cuts however small—without permission, they are breaking the law. And, perhaps more importantly, changing an artist's work. Please don't do that!

We are thrilled that this play has made it into your hands. We hope you love it as much as we do, and thank you for helping us keep the American theater alive and vital.

Note on Songs/Recordings, Images, or Other Production Design Elements

Be advised that Dramatists Play Service, Inc., neither holds the rights to nor grants permission to use any songs, recordings, images, or other design elements mentioned in the play. It is the responsibility of the producing theater/organization to obtain permission of the copyright owner(s) for any such use. Additional royalty fees may apply for the right to use copyrighted materials.

For any songs/recordings, images, or other design elements mentioned in the play, works in the public domain may be substituted. It is the producing theater/organization's responsibility to ensure the substituted work is indeed in the public domain. Dramatists Play Service, Inc., cannot advise as to whether or not a song/arrangement/recording, image, or other design element is in the public domain.